RUIN AND RESTORATION

D1566047

To suppose that God has a providential plan based on a special covenant with Israel and realised in the atonement presents us with a moral problem. In *Ruin and Restoration* David Martin sketches a radical naturalistic account of the atonement based on the innocent paying for the sins of the guilty through ordinary social processes.

An exercise in socio-theology, the book reflects on the contrast between 'the world' governed by the dynamic of violence as analysed by the social sciences, including international relations, and the emergence in Christianity (and Buddhism) of a non-violent alternative. A 'governing essay' fuses frameworks drawn from Reinhold Niebuhr, Karl Jaspers, Ernst Troeltsch and Max Weber and explores the relation between the cultural sciences, especially sociology, and theology treated as another but very distinctive cultural science. Six commentaries then deal with the atonement in detail; with the nature of Christian language and grammar, and with its characteristic mutations due to necessary compromises with 'the world'; with sex and violence; and with the liturgy as a concentrated mode of reconciliation.

David Martin is Emeritus Professor of Sociology, LSE, UK, and Fellow of the British Academy. He was born in Mortlake, in 1929 and attended East Sheen Grammar School and Westminster College, In the latter part of a seven year period in primary school teaching he took a first class (external) degree in sociology in his spare time and won a post-graduate scholarship to the LSE. He became a lecturer in the LSE sociology department in 1962 and professor from 1971–89. After his first book on Pacifism (1965) he produced the first critique of secularisation theory (1965) and the first statement of a general theory of secularisation (1969 and 1978). From 1986–90 he was distinguished professor of Human Values at Southern Methodist University and turned to the study of global Pentecostalism, producing, the first summary statement of the world-wide Pentecostal phenomenon in 1990. He also returned to the issue of religion and violence and explored issues in music and nationalism and sociology and theology. His intellectual autobiography *The Education of David Martin* appeared in 2013.

For my daughter Jessica, devoted parish priest:

Honorary Canon of Ely Cathedral; sometime Fellow of Trinity College,

Cambridge and Select Preacher to the University

Ruin and Restoration

On Violence, Liturgy and Reconciliation

DAVID MARTIN
London School of Economics, UK

Routledge
Taylor & Francis Group

LONDON AND NEW YORK

BT
265.
.M37
2016

First published 2016
by Routledge
2 Park Square, Milton Park, Abingdon, Oxon OX14 4RN

and by Routledge
711 Third Avenue, New York, NY 10017

Routledge is an imprint of the Taylor & Francis Group, an informa business

© 2016 David Martin

British Library Cataloguing in Publication Data
A catalogue record for this book is available from the British Library

Library of Congress Cataloging in Publication Data
Names: Martin, David, 1929–
Title: Ruin and restoration : on violence, liturgy, and reconciliation / by
    David Martin.
Description: Burlington : Ashgate, 2016. | Includes index.
Identifiers: LCCN 2015038066| ISBN 9781472480644 (hardcover) |
    ISBN 9781472480651 (pbk.) | ISBN 9781472483546 (ebook) |
    ISBN 9781472483553 (epub)
Subjects: LCSH: Atonement. | Religion and sociology.
Classification: LCC BT265.3 .M37 2016 | DDC 232/.3–dc23
LC record available at http://lccn.loc.gov/2015038066

ISBN: 9781472480644 (hbk)
ISBN: 9781472480651 (pbk)
ISBN: 9781315607108 (ebk)

Typeset in Garamond Premier Pro
by Apex CoVantage, LLC

Contents

Foreword

Charles Taylor

This is an extraordinarily rich book. It consists of a 'governing essay', followed by six 'commentaries', which bristle with new ideas and promising avenues of exploration. It is very difficult to do justice to it in a short description. But I'm going to try to give the gist of the main argument, at the price of some (I hope not too much) simplification.

I want to build the argument through four phases, or basic points, which I'll lay out in ascending order of depth, originality and eyebrow-lifting radicality.

1 The Grain of the World

The first starts from the obvious fact (once you think about it) that the central values or norms that we find preached and acted out in the Gospels – non-violence, universalism, self-sacrifice, service, repentance, reconciliation (p. 7) – could never be realised at the level of whole societies. They can be lived to the full by individuals, and also to some extent by small, dedicated groups, but not by entire political societies.

For instance, the Gospel calls for non-resistance to force, even when this is in the service of injustice. But societies that adopt total pacifism would rapidly fall victim to external conquest. It is not just that one couldn't in fact get everyone to adopt this stance voluntarily. It is also that dilemmas arise as soon as one proposes such a far-reaching change. Thus universal non-resistance in face of a threatening enemy that one could deter would have itself to be imposed by some sort of force. Or put another way, I could decide not to resist an aggressor, even to go to my death, but where this means that you too would be without defences, and you haven't chosen martyrdom, I would be failing you by not fighting back. As Martin says, there was nothing noble about our not intervening in the Rwandan massacre in the 1990s. Nor would we have been blameless if we had let the Yazidis suffer massacre and forced conversion at the hands of Islamic State.

There are restrictions built into our politico-moral predicament that set limits to our living the Gospel fully at the level of the collectivity, let alone the globe. The source of this resistance is what Martin calls 'the grain of the world'. Human beings live in societies, and cannot but do so. Societies need some sense of a 'we' or 'us', to which its members are bound. But the 'us' contrasts to a 'them'.

It would seem that at the dawn of humanity, this us/them partition was all-pervasive. The remarkable transformation in human history can perhaps be situated in the great Axial revolutions, which in one or another way introduce the notion of the human being as such, or of universal humanity, an idea with strong normative consequences. But these normative demands remain in tension with the ineradicable role of the us/them distinction in our lives.

Think of modern liberal democracy associated with the rule of law. It could be argued that this is the best (or least bad) regime that human history has thrown up (an example perhaps of the 'third way' of 'peaceable wisdom' of which Martin speaks in the Sixth Commentary). But democratic states need a strong sense of common allegiance, because they count on citizens doing what society requires (paying taxes, voting with some sense of the common good, perhaps serving in the army), without the coercion and threat that autocracies wield, and they need a high level of solidarity to survive. Free societies need 'patriotism', in other words, and this generally goes beyond (but includes) the 'constitutional' dimension which Habermas explores to encompass some historical, linguistic or ethnic markers. But these strong common bonds can be, on the one hand, the source of rivalries, sometimes leading to conflict (Putin's 'russky mir' vs. Ukraine), and on the other, they can generate cruel exclusions within wherever a segment of the population is deemed not to share the authentic national identity (see the rise of right-wing populism in Europe today).

The 'grain of the world' not only resists the full application of the Gospel, but is also an endless source of standing dilemmas and conundrums (e.g. how to have patriotism without exclusion, or how to realise the degree of equality democracies need without excessive coercion of the more fortunate. And so on).

Over against the Gospel values enumerated above, we find 'the inveterate struggle for dominance and the endlessly retributive honour codes associated with it' (p. 7). The grain of the world offers resistance to all the great Axial visions of the good; but not to all equally. Here Martin introduces a second key concept. Different Axial visions offer more or less acute 'axes of transcendence' to the world, measured by the extent and radicality of the demands they make on it.

For Martin, the most acute angle is to be found in Buddhism and Christianity. Relatively flatter angles can be seen, for instance, in Islam, or, in a rather different context, in Confucianism. Perhaps the key factor in high acuity is the stance towards violence. Christianity and Buddhism look forward to its total abandonment. And they also regard political power, rivalry, dominance, as practices to be transcended.

2 Sociology and Theology

The call to transcendence is a source of dilemmas, as we have seen. How to deal with these? How to understand them theologically?

First, how to deal with them. Here we come to the issues which Vatican II described as 'reading the signs of the times'. It is possible to go wrong here in either direction: either to be too pusillanimous and complacent in accepting unjust and inhuman regimes and practices (Christian Churches until the eighteenth century in regard to slavery; the Catholic Church until recently in relation to democracy). Or we can be too unrealistic and 'utopian' in endorsing radical change (some twentieth-century Christians in relation to Communism and Fascism).

What one needs in order to gauge the signs of the times is a combination of different ways of understanding, which can be roughly identified with the disciplines of theology, sociology and history.

It is relevant to mention here the extraordinary triple competence of David Martin in these domains, to which he adds a deep grasp of western music and the history of literature and art. There is a small group of social scientists with this triple competence who have helped revolutionise our understanding of both faith and history: Robert Bellah and Martin in an older generation, Hans Joas and José Casanova in a younger cohort, to whom we could add Craig Calhoun. These also have drawn on Ernst Troeltsch and Max Weber, as well as Karl Jaspers. (Martin also mentions Niebuhr.) In future, people will be astonished that theologians proposed reading the signs of the times without reference to the sister disciplines (as the Roman Catholic magisterium did until recently).

Martin goes further in showing the important analogies and overlappings between theology and sociology. He is speaking, of course, of a hermeneutic sociology, informed by history, not of the vain and sterile attempts to imitate natural science in the search for invariant 'laws'. In this sense, sociology englobes history, and we can speak of a double, rather than triple competence.

In a sense, sociology (in this meaning) and theology between them map the tensions between the highest Axial demands and the grain of the world. But this is not just a matter of theology defining the demands and sociology delineating the resistant grain of things. There is a closer analogy between the two. Sociology operates with its own, often implicit, normative concepts: it speaks of norm and deviancy, functional versus dysfunctional, of the requirements for the proper operation of certain systems (as I did above in talking about modern democracy needing strong bonds). And as an inevitable consequence it also explores possible changes for the better.

A sociology that wants to negate faith (Weber?) still defines a horizon of feasible transformation (how to avoid/mitigate the 'iron cage') that can guide our action. The two disciplines operate in the same sphere, are playing in the same sandbox, as it were. So they can't help bumping into each other, which is why you need the double (triple) competence to play here.

One of the great merits of this book is to have pointed this out, shocking as the news will be for many practitioners in each discipline. (Eyebrows rising on both sides.)

Another way of understanding the analogy, complementarity and/or rivalry between the two is to see how we are all heirs of the Axial revolutions, in some form or other. Individuals may profess different degrees of disabused cynicism, but almost no one espouses openly and consciously a non-universalist ethic. (The role of unconscious hypocrisy and bias is another matter.) Nazism was the great exception that makes the rule stand out. One might almost invert Niebuhr's famous title (moral man vs. immoral society): cynical individuals profess a demanding social ethic. Our great divisions across the field of theistic and anti-theistic positions concern the direction, scope and conditions of possible ethical transformations.

3 Sin

That being said, the crucial thesis of the book is Martin's theological reading of our condition, that is, of our incapacity to realise the full demands of the Gospel. We speak of this incapacity in terms of sin. This incapacity is accompanied by another, which we might speak of as a limitation. We are mortal, and subject to various infirmities of the flesh. Let's speak for short of incapacity and infirmity.

One reading, which links both, and has been very powerful in our Christian tradition, is that incapacity is the result of an original moral fault (expressed in the crucial story of the disobedient eating of the apple). This is taken to mean that the incapacity is something we morally deserve. To this is added the notion that the infirmity is a consequence of the acquired incapacity; it is, we might say, a punishment for the fault. These two theses often go together with an account of the atonement as effective reparation to God for the fault (which only the Son of God could make), which lifts the punishment.

Martin rejects this as a morally inacceptable moralisation of the incapacity, which draws on a reading of the history of Israel frequently invoked in the Old Testament, whereby flourishing was the fruit of obedience to God's Law, and its infringement brought about the terrible consequences of defeat, exile and captivity.

Instead he offers what he calls a 'naturalistic explanation' of this incapacity. It is rooted in the grain of our world, as we emerge as homo sapiens from the evolutionary process. Incapacity and also infirmity are in this sense natural phenomena.

But explaining incapacity is not yet explaining sin. Incapacity is the locus of sin only in the context of God's call to us to transform and be transformed. Thus sin or sinfulness becomes a more complex concept, if I understand Martin correctly. It has two inextricably intertwined dimensions. It is on one level our starting condition. Outside the perspective of faith, it would remain just this. But within this perspective, we see this incapacity as a limit which God offers to bring us beyond. The atonement is the act wherein God takes on himself the destruction, the inflicted injustice and the disfigurement, which is the inevitable result of the incapacity as it works itself out in human history. This is both a revelation of our sorry reality and an act that opens a way beyond it. That is, it opens a way to the potential full realisation of the demands of the Gospel, by healing the deep divisions that the incapacity generates. It both makes manifest our divisions and reconciles them.

This opens the second dimension of sinfulness, inseparable from the first, but notionally distinct. In this dimension, sin is resistance to this revealing/healing power, the refusal we find in ourselves to follow it, to go along with it.

(Perhaps there is also a third dimension, or another way of responding to the distance between our condition and God's call. This is the response of radical evil: to seek integrity and wholeness in a total rejection of God's healing reconciliation, in the giddy rapture of violence and destruction. As Dostoevsky showed, only a creature who experiences the call to go beyond our incapacity could feel the temptation to this transcendence through radical evil. This is a plausible reading of much that we see in our contemporary world.)

4 Liturgy

Sin as resistance to God's call (and even more, sin as radical evil) collapses the (felt) tension between our incapacity and the pull of God's healing, either by normalising the incapacity or by projecting a response to it that is entirely in our power. The tension has to be kept alive: by keeping alive the eschatological vision, by constant pushing against the limits that the grain of things imposes, seeking the signs of the times, by special vocations: of charity, healing, contemplation, prayer. But a special place falls to liturgy.

The healing of atonement is prolonged in liturgy. The revelation-reconciliation of the atonement is at work in history, not in some form of continuous progress, but as mustard seeds which grow into the great trees we live among. And one of the crucial ways that these grow and constitute the unseen environment of our world is through liturgy.

***

I have tried in the above to sketch out what I (hopefully not too distortively) perceive as the basic thrust of Martin's argument. This will be shocking to many, but it offers a way of linking theology to history and experience which opens large and important avenues of future development.

I have tried to follow the main lines, incorporating points both in the 'governing essay' and in the commentaries. But I should add a few words about these latter, because they are full of very rich and fertile insights.

The First Commentary offers a full account of the theological notions I sketched in section 3 above. In particular what is arresting here is the explanation of the phrase in the Easter Preface of 'felix culpa', and the reading of the resurrection stories in terms of the restoration of table fellowship. This helps us to understand the crucial place Martin gives to liturgy.

The Second Commentary develops the argument against sin as something we generate by bad action, deserving of punishment.

The Third Commentary deals with issues of family, of the relation of sex and violence, and of the erotic to the aesthetic.

The Fourth Commentary discusses the attempts to go beyond violence which often generate their own eschatological violence. It contains a very interesting discussion of liberal internationalism and its efforts to convince us that we have the means ourselves to bring an end to violence in a good world order, an outlook that Martin argues is profoundly illusory.

The Fifth Commentary offers a tremendously rich account of modern music and poetry, and the return in force within it of the idea and model of liturgy. Martin's deep knowledge and understanding in this field is deployed to great effect. This section is full of mind-changing insights. It invites you again and again to stop and go for a long walk to work out their implications. By itself it is worth the price of admission.

The Sixth Commentary speaks of a 'third way' of peaceable wisdom, which I invoked in the discussion of section 1.

If I could riff a bit on this, I would say that this book shows what a strange and paradoxical animal the human being is. In two dimensions: our history really does show something like progress or improvement – first in the rise of the Axial visions of the good, which go way beyond our original condition and then in this ability to develop 'least bad' regimes', such as democracy, the rule of law, Confucian rule at its best and so on; while at the same time, we have a lamentable inability to sustain over time even these 'least bad' forms, let alone to introduce them successfully over wide parts of the globe. We evade this paradox through dreams of 'progress', either achieved or on the verge of achievement. How can an animal dream of, even commit itself to, such perfections which go so much 'against its grain'? Some of the best answers to this question are perhaps theological. The germ of one such is in this remarkable book.

Acknowledgements

The 'governing essay' began life as a lecture prepared in 2014 in honour of Klaus Tanner's 60th birthday at Heidelberg University, but read for me on account of my absence through grave family illness. A variant of it, revised for the purposes of the theme of 'implicit religion', appeared in the journal *Implicit Religion* in 2015 at the kind instance of the late Edward Bailey (*Implicit Religion*, 18(2) (2015): 159–75). The version printed here is a very much expanded revision of the original lecture, given at a conference on Sociology and Theology at the John Paul the Second Centre in Warsaw on 2 June 2015 and posted on the Centre's website. An earlier exploration of some of the themes was published as 'Axial Religions and the Problem of Violence' in the collection of essays on *The Axial Age and its Consequences* edited by Robert Bellah and Hans Joas (Harvard University/Belknap Press, 2012, pp. 294–316). A parallel discussion of the themes in the Fifth Commentary focused on the theme of the return of the sacred in 'classical' music appeared in *The Wiley-Blackwell Companion to World Christianity*, edited by Michael McClymond and Lamin Sanneh (forthcoming in February 2016). My overall argument is anticipated in my chapter, 'A Relational Ontology Reviewed in Sociological Perspective', in *The Trinity and an Entangled World: Relationality in Physical Science and Theology*, edited by John Polkinghorne (Eerdmans, 2010).

I have only occasionally footnoted the very numerous quotations, usually by memory, from the KJV of the English Bible.

Vergnügte Ruh, beliebte Seelenlust (Blessed peace, beloved desire of the soul)
(J.S. Bach cantata 170 for Trinity 6)

> *Tu del ciel minstro eletto*
> *non vedrai piu nel mio petto*
> *volgia infida, o vano ardor.*
> *E se vissi ingrate a Dio*
> *tu custode del cor mio*
> *a lui port ail nuovo cor.*
>
> (You, high minister of Heaven
> shall see no more in my heart
> a faithless wish or empty craving
> And though I lived unmindful of God
> may you, as guardian of my heart,
> Bring to Him a heart made new.)

G.F. Handel, *Il Trionfo del Tempo e del Disinganno*, Libretto by Benedetto Pamphili, translation by Anthony Hicks: the final aria of *Belleza*.

Introduction

This book traverses territory that arouses political sensitivities, and excites prohibitions or inhibitions on what may be said in public on pain of scholarly excommunication. I therefore need to be clear concerning positions about which some of my most admired friends might be unhappy. With regard to Judaism, I have had a long association in England, America and Israel with Jewish colleagues. In the course of that association I have the impression, no more, that Evangelical Christians, especially maybe those in the philosemitic tradition best known and native to me, immerse themselves in the Hebrew Bible, apart from the Torah, far more than comparably committed Jews. One devout Jew asked me where I had come across the beautiful sentiment about doing justly and loving mercy that Christians regularly quote from the prophet Micah. Another devout Jew commented on his intense dislike of Isaiah, the prophet that Christians call the fifth evangelist. Reading different Bibles differently is only one source of the many misunderstandings between Christians and Jews. We misunderstand each other while seeking with strenuous goodwill to acquire understanding.

My problem is that I find the idea of a special providential relationship between God and a particular people, or just particular individual people, morally dubious. It is a politically useful myth assisting survival and morale, just as its secular equivalents, like Fate, Destiny (manifest or otherwise) and Social Darwinism are useful myths. I object comprehensively to every variant of teleological history, and the deleterious lumber associated with all of them, whether Jewish in the seventh century bc, Islamic in the seventh century ad or Marxist, Hegelian or Whig in the nineteenth century. If that is a 'phobia' I openly embrace it and it may well have its origins in my reading of Karl Popper in the 1950s.

I find the character of a God micro-managing history for a particular people's benefit, including their moral benefit, morally dubious to the point where I see this God, or this aspect of him, as a projection deserving Blake's epithet 'Old Nobodaddy'. My distaste for, say, the Book of Joshua in the Hebrew Bible, grows even more emphatic when I encounter the God of the Koran. This supposedly perfect revelation, while mostly evading the critical scholarship applied to the Bible by Christians and others for over two hundred years, clearly endorses violence, whatever it also says about 'no compulsion in religion'. That revulsion has to be set in the context of my basic assumption that all ideologies and religions, not excluding those founded on texts forbidding violence, will, in practice, find justifications for violent action that reflect the violence written into human society as such, sometimes with considerable enthusiasm.

Communism, nationalism, Islam, established Christianity, established Buddhism and Judaism have all practised violence, given the chance, notably against minorities and dissenters. The practice of violence is not, as some pretend, especially characteristic of religion, unless you redefine religion to cover all ideologies from North Korea to Pol Pot and Stalin to suit your polemic purposes. It seems to me that for Buddhism and Christianity the justification of violence involves a greater degree of tension with normative texts than in the case of either Judaism or Islam. That is why I regard the notion of the 'Abrahamic religions' as a useful political construct that conceals the remarkable extent to which Christianity differs from either Islam or Judaism, in spite of its overwhelming debt to the latter. I hope no reader supposes I am unaware of the achievements of cultures associated with Islam both in the promotion of science and the exercise of semi-tolerance in particular eras. That is another issue.

I also hope against hope it is not necessary to say that when I note that the Koran frequently enjoins violence, and that Islam has its own version of 'In this sign conquer', I do *not* therefore suppose for one moment that most Muslims are violent. That should be obvious. At the same time I do not ignore the writings of serious commentators who suppose that Islam, as a religion spread initially by astonishing military achievements, has a natural affinity for super-ordinate status as a majority. Christianity by contrast is a religion that spent three centuries as an intermittently oppressed minority, and understood martyrdom as the warfare of the cross not as death in physical *jihad*. That experience informed its character before it had its chance as a state religion eventually constituting a majority and before Constantine wrenched a politically convenient meaning out of 'In this sign conquer'.

Beyond all that, I see no reason to suppose that non-Muslims are in a position to declare, sometimes for political reasons as in the case of President Obama, that the extraordinarily violent manifestations of Islamism are not authentically Islamic, given that Islamist theologians and ideological spokesmen can cite so many texts supporting their position. The history of Baghdad, city of peace and blood, shows that there is nothing specifically contemporary or historically unusual about such manifestations of appalling violence. Obama and others even declare, against all the evidence, that no 'real religion' behaves like this. 'Real' religions have done and continue to do precisely this. Buddhism in Burma and Sri Lanka persecutes enthusiastically, though any responsible social scientist will analyse the ubiquitous 'secular' power drives at work. Perhaps I need also to say that Islam, like all major religions, entertains a vast variety of different schools of thought, some of which reject the Islamist use of violent *jihad*. All that I take for granted.

Of course, those engaged in the pursuit of violence, of whatever faith or ideology, can and do cite justifications. Justifications are always to hand as 'secular' political drives require. The inverted commas around 'secular' simply indicate my assumption that what Christianity calls 'the world' is like that. Justifications are available, whether or not the angle of transcendence is maximal or minimal. In the case of Christianity and Buddhism it is maximal to the point where justifications are very much harder to come by, but they are always available as needed. As I point out in the text, Jesus represents a maximal angle of transcendence by being neither a war leader nor having a family and by seeking a kingdom 'not of this world'. I am reminded of the Crusader who was visited with the idea that the Gospels forbade his participation, and had to be assured by the Pope that his conscientious scruples could be set on one side, given current political exigencies. As they say, 'needs must when the Devil drives', and especially when the alternative could well have been, as Gibbon noted, that Islam was taught in the divinity schools of Oxford.

My scholarly approach is broadly Weberian, especially with regard to the tensions with 'the world' that salvation religions with marked angles of transcendence generate in the aesthetic, economic and political spheres. That is especially the case in what is for me the crucial matter of recourse to violence. But this is not an exercise in Weberian scholarship. Similarly, I assume acquaintance with the vast corpus of critical scholarship on the Bible, which began for me with Schweitzer and Loisy and continues today with many writers, including my friend Bart Ehrmann. I know the kind of arguments adduced by Richard Bauckham concerning eye-witness accounts lying behind the Gospels and the greatly diminished usefulness of Albert Schweitzer's approach. I happen to think, as against the historical sceptics, that the main emphases of the Gospels are surprisingly clear, not to say disconcerting. But this text is no more a survey of literature on the Bible than it is an exercise in Weberian scholarship. With specific regard to the atonement as one of my major themes, I do not engage with recent theological debates. Rather I explore what would be involved in a naturalistic understanding of the atonement quite distinct from all extant theories.

This book is a disciplinary hybrid you might call socio-theology. The governing essay at the beginning understands Christianity and Buddhism as the 'axial religions' most obviously against 'the grain of the world' with respect to sex and violence and therefore opposed to the rivalrous dynamics of politics within states or between them. Inevitably both religions must compromise with 'the world'. They split into those versions that reject violence and other versions that collude with it in alliance with other social formations. They may closely collude with it, as the Catholic Church did in the great military orders of the late Middle Ages, or as contemporary Buddhist monks do in Burma and Sri Lanka. I identify an oscillation within Christianity between setting up 'the kingdom' by violence and inserting the seeds of 'the kingdom' within us and within culture to fructify far from their point of origin. This fructification often occurs well outside the boundaries of the Church and well beyond the confines of 'Christian' culture. They are in a profound sense extra-mural. Much of this has been the substance of my sociological work over half a century and more.

The governing essay traces the tension between 'the kingdom' and 'the world' and therefore traces the tension between the social sciences as accounts of how 'the world' works in practice, and Christianity as a hope concerning a better world. The chasm between 'the kingdom' and 'the world' can only be bridged at great cost and the governing essay considers some of the ways that cost is or is not paid.

The six commentaries take up themes touched upon in the governing essay: roughly they are on sin and primal violence and the meaning of atonement (p. 27); on the grammar and vocabulary of 'Speaking Christian' (p. 41); on sex, the family and universal love (p. 57); on the quest for peace and the reality of violence (p. 71); on the return of the liturgical and the search for reconciliation with musical and poetic modernism (p. 81); and on the peaceable mediation of Wisdom (p. 99). The Afterword sums up and spells out the wider implications of the argument and concludes by bringing together the thematic repertoire of Christianity in its confrontation with 'the world'. I take up themes originally broached but not always carried through in my book *The Breaking of the Image* (1980) and I develop some earlier work on the complex relation of music to secularisation compared with the somewhat simpler story in the plastic arts.

In the course of this book I have drawn intellectual and imaginative sustenance from discussions with my daughter, and from listening to her sermons. Throughout all my writing my overwhelming debt is to Bernice and, specifically in this book, to her ideas about appropriate illustrations. Again and again she has held or guided my hand intellectually and otherwise when I have faltered in the face of a particularly knotty problem or difficult transition.

David Martin
June 2015

Governing Essay

Sociology and Theology: With and Against the Grain of 'the World'

Preliminaries: Fusing Weber, Jaspers, Troeltsch and Niebuhr

My theme is the nature of the interface of sociology and theology, and I focus on four scholars working within German intellectual traditions: Ernst Troeltsch, Max Weber, Karl Jaspers and Reinhold Niebuhr. I suggest that sociology is close to theology in its narrative and historically contingent character, and in its evident ideological loadings. At the same time sociology is dangerous to theology because it embraces a different dialectic between what is and what might be. In theology this dialectic is only in part expressed in theoretical constructions, for example the writing of Reinhold Niebuhr, in *Moral Man and Immoral Society* (1932), by which this chapter is greatly influenced, though I think Niebuhr's contrast between the possibilities of moralisation at the large-scale collective level and enhanced possibilities at the intra-personal level over-dramatised.[1] Alongside theory, theology works paradigmatically within a framework of condensed stories, such as the primal murder of Abel by Cain, the great dramas of exile and return, and the confrontation of 'kingdom' with 'world' in the Gospels, and between integrity and *real-politik* in the narrative of the Passion.

I fuse frameworks derived from Weber and Jaspers as well as Troeltsch and Reinhold Niebuhr. My analysis rests initially on Max Weber, notably his formulation of 'religious rejections' of the world in all the major spheres of social existence, the political, economic, erotic, aesthetic,[2] and on Karl Jasper's notion

---

[1]   The political problem of forgiving your enemies at the expense of truthfulness and treason to your friends is scarcely less acute at the intra-personal level.

[2]   The aesthetic tension is only occasionally touched on in this book but I was early introduced to it by writers a long way from the concerns of sociology. I do not suppose that Violet Markham had an interest in Weber but in her book *Romanesque France* (London: John Murray, 1929) she discusses the 'miracle' of Christian art, given the background of a religious rejection of representation. Cistercian art in particular rejects representation through sculpture. Nevertheless, Cistercian austerity breeds beauty. Moreover, Cistercian *askesis* breeds an anthropology of desire derived from a symbolic reading of the erotic in

of an Axial Age around the first millennium bc. I integrate the Axial revolutions of that first millennium with the 'religious rejections', and I treat the nascent 'world religions' as involving very different 'angles of transcendence', minimal in China and Islam, maximal in primitive Christianity and classical Buddhism. By 'angle of transcendence' I mean the degree to which a religion, or in the case of Greece and China, a type of philosophic understanding, posits a mode of transformation, which in some cases radically revises the brutal dynamics of ordinary existence, or seeks to harmonise them much less radically in the image of some ideal order. In this perspective the diacritical markers are not between the Abrahamic religions, so-called, and the rest, but between primitive Christianity and classical Buddhism, and the rest.

Crucially I take for granted as integral to a realist view the violent struggle in all complex societies and between them over scarce goods. That struggle is equally basic in sociology, political science, international relations and biology. These two *assumptions*, first about religious rejections, rephrased as varying '*angles of transcendence*', and second, about the inveterate struggle over scarce goods, have to be taken *together*. Once that is done, the key criterion of difference (and one cognate with the critical difference I postulate between Christianity and Buddhism, and the rest) is the attitude towards and understanding of violence.

I now focus on Christianity, both in its original radical form and in its adapted imperial and national forms, and on the tension between faith and social reality, above all the social reality of violence. This tension underlies the Christian concept of 'the world' set over against 'the kingdom', and the Augustinian distinction between the City of God and the City of Man. In that basic Augustinian distinction Christianity codes the tension between violence as that is expressed in the struggle over scarce goods and the struggle for domination, and its eschatological hopes for peace and unity rooted in faith and love. But the social reality of *real-politik* and the dire necessities of statecraft are only explicitly formulated in the early modern period, for example by Machiavelli, although theorists of international relations trace the basic principles of statecraft back to understandings of shifting alliances and pre-emptive warfare formulated by Thucydides in his *History of the Peloponnesian War*. The fundamental dynamics and inveterate struggles of the social order, I refer to as 'the grain of the world', adopting a phrase from the pacifist theologian Stanley Hauerwas. I argue that Christianity is against 'the grain of the world'. My expectation would be that theologians prefer to think in terms of a basic harmony understood as with 'the

---

the Song of Songs as discussed in Michael Casey, *A Thirst for God* (Kalamazoo: Cistercian Publications, 1988).

grain of the world' rather than in terms of a fundamental violence understood as part of the dialectic of Us and Them.

Since writing on *Pacifism*[3] fifty years ago, I treat the issue of peace and violence as a critical marker of the manner in which religious rejections, notably in Christianity and Buddhism, introduce into human language an alternative discourse based on non-violence, universalism, self-sacrifice, service, repentance and reconciliation, not on the inveterate struggle for dominance and the endlessly retributive honour codes associated with it. That happens to be the Christian formulation, but a similar alternative discourse also emerges in Buddhism. Given the existence of acute social pressure to conform to the 'grain of the world', faiths like Christianity and Buddhism will devise compromises with it, partly suppressing the original template of radical non-violence.

The foundational narrative of non-violence will persist as a cultural undertow protected and enabled to survive and fructify by the concept of the sacred, and by the reproductive institutional capacities of the Church, more especially in liturgy and the text of the New Testament. In liturgy the alternative discourse of repentance, reconciliation and peace will be re-enacted, and moreover this discourse will taken up 'extra-murally' as the basis for a critique of the Church's corruption by 'the world'. That is conspicuously the case with regard to contemporary pacifism, which is not strictly a rejection of violence as such, but a pacific presumption taking off from suppressed and half-forgotten Christian premises admixed with ideas derived from India in the nineteenth century through the colonial experience. The result can be an embrace of the Christian rejection of 'the world', especially with regard to violence, for example in Leo Tolstoy and Benjamin Britten. But one also finds this 'Christian' rejection embraced by large swathes of the contemporary intelligentsia, accepting the Christian narrative as a given, but not counting the full cost of non-violent sacrifice. Non-violence is not necessarily the 'nicer' or easier alternative understood according to some utilitarian calculus, although if it stands a chance it is a preferred option, as in the Civil Rights movement led by Martin Luther King. There was nothing morally impressive in non-intervention in Rwanda. I mean that non-violence *can* be even more costly than violence, and that cost is built into liturgy in the sign of the broken and humiliated body of the Saviour. The cost of non-violence and integrity is placarded before our eyes at Golgotha and re-enacted wherever bread is broken in the ciborium and wine poured into

---

[3]   David Martin, *Pacifism: An Historical and Sociological Study*, London: Routledge, 1965.

the chalice. Liturgy tells the truth about endemic violence and in the moment of the sharing of gifts effects reconciliation.

In summary, I assume an irresolvable tension between the pressure of the Christian narrative to achieve peace and unity, and the social reality of brokenness and division, dramatically illustrated in the capacity of the Eucharist as a sacrament of unity to be itself a crux of conflict. The Eucharist is, of course, eschatological in that it looks forward to Christ's kingdom of peace. Moreover, the hopes of all who implicitly talk as though universal peace is possible are also eschatological. Secular and religious hopes are alike eschatological. As already indicated, I take a 'realist' Niebuhrian position. I maintain that the Christian narrative embodies a dialectic between visions of peace and the profoundly resistant realities of the social order.[4] One of my main pieces of evidence will be the various negotiating stratagems adopted by the Church when Christianity is embraced by members of the senatorial class in the late Roman Empire, in part to evade the implications of Christ's radical view of the spiritual dangers and corruptions of riches. Again, much contemporary religion seems by implication to endorse this critique, just as it appears to endorse the critique of violence. I mean that large swathes of the commentariat and of ecclesiastical opinion gesture in the direction of peace without embracing the logic of pacifism. It would be *nice* if we could evade the crux.

The Argument

I begin the main body of the argument by elaborating my basic assumptions. When I refer to sociology I include all the cultural disciplines such as politics, cultural anthropology and some versions of psychology. When I refer to theology I largely restrict myself to Christianity and I focus on Christianity as a variety of symbolic logic, a condensed sign language with a coherent grammar. This symbolic logic or sign language codes an acute angle of transcendence on a 'world' of 'principalities and powers' that resists the rule of God or 'the kingdom'. Nevertheless the world is *in principle* capable of being remade in the divine image. That tension between the way of the world and re-creation lies at the heart of my argument.

I assume the cultural disciplines have a logical structure that differs from the model of natural science. That is obviously true of theology but it is also true of

---

4   Stanley Hauerwas, *With the Grain of the Universe: The Church's Witness and Natural Theology*, Grand Rapids, MI: Baker, 2001.

all the cultural disciplines, and I need to explore the character of the cultural disciplines before I can juxtapose sociology and theology. Science, understood as a way of knowing, is pursued in different ways according to the subject matter. There are many modes of knowing along a spectrum from 'explanation' in natural science to 'understanding' in the cultural disciplines, from data to what Alfred Schütz called 'capta'.

The cultural disciplines, theology included alongside sociology, depend on history. History involves narrative, and narrative involves contingency and subjectivity. By contingency I mean that if the Germans had not been motivated to help Lenin on his way to the Finland Station vast tracts of subsequent history might have been different. History can only be narrated in ordinary language in principle available to any competent language user. The same applies to the cultural disciplines. They have no concepts like 'quasars' in astrophysics or even 'metabolism' in medicine, unless metabolism is used metaphorically. The fundamental role played by contingent narrative expressed in ordinary language means that the cultural disciplines are metaphorical and rhetorical to a degree not found in the natural sciences, and they proliferate taxonomies. They sprawl, because attended by numerous qualifications dependent on cultural time and space. The setting out of the *ceteris paribus* clause can be very extended indeed.

That means that the cultural sciences are wordy and full of what Clifford Geertz called 'thick description'; and the semantic aura of words means that the concepts seemingly deployed by practitioners of the cultural sciences as the manipulable counters of tightly organised argument resist reduction to bounded entities. This in turn means that (say) a postulated relationship between length of time in political power and increasing corruption resists reduction to equations. The cultural disciplines are not inadequate attempts to apply the methods of the natural sciences, complete with their manipulation of variables through controlled experiments, universal generalisations and (other things being equal), ability to predict. They emphatically do not accept the protocols of naturalistic reductionism as those are criticised by Hans Joas in *Faith as an Option*.[5]

Just because the cultural disciplines, sociology in particular, share characteristics with theology they are both relevant and dangerous to it. But I have not quite exhausted the similarities. The cultural disciplines are very prone to revisit their classics for insight. We often call ourselves Weberians, Marxists or Durkheimians in spite of the distance that some believe separates us from the great pioneers of the subject in the nineteenth and early twentieth centuries.

[5]   Hans Joas, *Faith as an Option: Possible Futures for Christianity*, Stanford: Stanford University Press, 2014.

Ibn Khaldun and Giambattista Vico remain our contemporaries. We are not latecomers to the scientific enterprise waiting for a revolutionary Isaac Newton but inheritors of a long and essentially cumulative tradition of observation. Machiavelli's *The Prince* was the nearest we came to a scientific revolution *and it remains* the founding text of political sociology. The objections to *The Prince* that convulsed Europe even more than Darwin's *The Origin of Species* were moral objections based on its obvious truth not on its falsity. It defines what I mean by realism. The cultural disciplines are, *like theology*, cumulative rather than revolutionary. Sociologists, *like theologians*, revisit their canonical texts.

I make just one or two more preliminary observations. One relates to what I said about the obvious truth of Machiavelli's *The Prince*. What Machiavelli describes is universal in developed societies and maybe universal wherever two or at any rate three people are gathered together. This tells us that 'the obvious' can be practised for aeons without anyone articulating it. But maybe the obvious was articulated long ago in stories: Cain and Abel, scheming Jacob and naive Esau, Sarah and her handmaid Hagar. Maybe a story is the most concentrated form of truth telling we have. We shall return to this when we discuss theology because theology not only tells the truth through stories but the truth it offers is *telling*: it strikes home. Meanwhile I note that the obvious is only obvious retrospectively. Up to 1513 politics had been seen through the lens of classical humanism based on the trustworthiness of the honourable man and on Christian loving-kindness. Renaissance Italy easily recognised itself portrayed in *The Prince* and it also recognised this description was simultaneously a prescription about what was required if one wanted to rule. Machiavelli argued that to achieve this desired end or result you needed to use these means; it was the law of political survival which could just as well be *for* the common good as a conspiracy *against* it. You had to do evil to achieve collective good as well as collective harm. Caiaphas put it very succinctly in the story of the Passion: 'It is *expedient* one die for the people.' As a practice Caiaphas understood realism in ad 33 as well as Machiavelli understood it intellectually in 1513.

Emphatically I reject the historically 'progressive' notion that in the course of a transition from early modern times to the present we have shifted from religious idealisations obscurely wrapped in myth to realistic political philosophies shorn of myth and based on a 'rationalised' world view. On the contrary, though a philosophy like liberalism may embody an internally coherent set of political and philosophic *principles*, the liberal account of the workings of the world is a mythic projection. The hopes of those who greeted the Arab Spring as a blissful dawn in which corruption might be relegated to the unregenerate past and in which (as Wordsworth said of the French Revolution) it was 'very heaven' to be alive, were hardly based on sober likelihoods. Social myths have analogues in myths about Nature, and Wordsworth again offers telling examples in the *Lyrical Ballads* of 1798 and *The Prelude* of 1805. As he says in the 1798 Preface his responses to the world and to Nature represent 'the spontaneous overflow of powerful feelings'.[6]

The cultural sciences easily fuse description and prescription, the empirical and the moral, what ought to be and what is. What Machiavelli described and prescribed was morally corrupt, and corruption is a fundamental concept in political science and political sociology. What is true of Machiavelli as the founder of political science is equally true of Marx, Weber, Spencer and Durkheim as the modern founders of sociology. Their texts embed a moral perspective. I am not denying for a moment that the cultural sciences also seek objectivity and *Wertfreiheit*, but their objectivity and value freedom is enhanced by, and depends on, full recognition of the role of perspective and moral standpoint. Of course, social scientists must face up to the implications of the data, however shocking these may be, and the realism I refer to in this essay relies on extremely shocking observation. I do not for a moment deny that social scientists seek regular relationships where possible and trace causal sequences which can sometimes be expressed in quantitative comparisons according to the logic of statistics. But they are characteristically and by the nature of their subject matter committed observers scrutinising what is, in order both to understand, and to descry, what might be.

The fact that the cultural sciences embed moral perspectives has paradoxical consequences. When quasi-objective concepts in the cultural sciences are transferred to everyday speech, often to give them the objective aura associated with science, they acquire the force of moral judgements. To describe individual behaviour as 'pathological' or institutional practices as 'dysfunctional' is to make a covert moral judgement. The ethical is built in and so is the critical. Sociology is a critical discipline. But the ethical and the critical are not built in as quasars are built into physics and metabolism into medicine. They are built in on account of the necessity of human choice.

I have suggested that sociology and the humanities generally embed moral perspectives on account of choice. Such perspectives are also embedded on account of the inevitable deployment of forms of ordinary speech replete with moral loadings that are the intimate coinage of any competent language user.[7]

---

[6] Stephen Prickett, *Religion and Romanticism: The Tradition of Coleridge and Wordsworth in the Victorian Church*, Cambridge: Cambridge University Press, 1970.

[7] Rowan Williams, *The Edge of Words and the Habits of Language*, London: Bloomsbury Continuum, 2014.

That is quite adequately controversial though it is conceded by numerous practitioners of the cultural and hermeneutic sciences. But one can go further and suggest that ordinary language embeds moral perspectives in a way that has even more controversial implications. Consider my earlier observation at the beginning of this governing essay about the dilemma posed by forgiving one's enemies at the expense of treason to one's friends and of the truth. This is an obvious enough observation about collective behaviour insofar as the politician who openly 'forgives' those of the opposite party is soon defined as a traitor, but the observation holds equally for personal relationships. Forgiveness and reconciliation depend in all situations, collective and personal alike, on telling at least the substantial truth, if not the whole truth, otherwise the supposed closure exemplifies 'cheap grace'. 'Cheap grace' is not simply part of theological discourse but present generically in human experience, which is to say that theological as well as moral categories are embedded in observation of human interaction as such.[8]

Observation of what is involved in everyday dilemmas lies at the heart of sociological understanding: it is inherent in any quest to *understand* the dilemmas and basic processes of living with others through a methodology based on experiential and controlled insight. For this methodology the experiential *is* the empirical. Sociology is about the corruption that attends our projects and about the cost of recognising the wounds, the damage and the harm they trail in the longer term but which we initially prefer not to contemplate. It seeks to probe the nature of agency (or choice), to identify the sources of culpability and of what John Ruskin (in *Munera Pulveris*) called 'wealth' and 'illth', and to name victimhood wherever it is to be found. Even in the apparently mundane sphere of social policy and administration, a subject that claims in the name of science to supersede 'going about doing good', an innocuous formulation such as 'unintended consequences' covers everything from variables that could not be known in advance of contingent events, or were known but screened out, or deliberately suppressed in case they interfered with the overriding aim by drawing attention to likely costs. Corruption and cost, culpability and victimhood, are moral categories that carry profound theological loadings. The Gospels turn paradigmatically on the losses we suffer on account of corruption and on the cost of redemption. Sociologists are unwitting theologians who prefer to work at a safe 'objective' distance from their subject matter so that sociological texts require very close reading to reveal their buried roots in excoriating and shocking

---

8   See the discussion of Dietrich Bonhoeffer in Gregory Jones, *Embodying Forgiveness: A Theological Analysis*, Grand Rapids, MI: Eerdmans, 1995.

experience. To the extent that theologians and literary scholars occupy a middle distance that enables them to come up close to excoriating lived experience of the logic and dynamic of situations, for example in Shakespeare's late plays, their moral and theological projects are relatively transparent.

Belief in the natural science model, as of universal application and as defining what is to count as science, is not scientific. It is philosophy, and dubious philosophy at that. We are dealing with variants of positivism, and it is the diffuse influence of positivism among politicians that requires the cultural sciences to deform themselves on the natural science model. The suspicion of the cultural sciences, especially sociology, currently rife among the educated public, and the similar suspicion of theology, derive from this vulgar positivism. Nevertheless there are practitioners of the cultural sciences who embrace positivism with suspicious fervour as though seeking to compensate for what they fear may be a lack. Moreover, practitioners of social science recognise a shifting frontier with natural science and that bears on how the cultural sciences relate to theology. In the early twentieth century the frontiers of culture, understood as infinitely varied and open to transformation, were advanced at the expense of the data of biology defining what was universal and unalterable. Whether or not this was true it was defended for reasons rooted in a political commitment to change. In the late twentieth century this shift was reversed in favour of the unalterable givens of biology by way of evolutionary psychology or cognitive science. We overhear this shift when people say it's 'in the DNA' or 'hard-wired'.

The exact location of the frontier does not matter here *unless* it is claimed that the space of the cultural disciplines, including theology, will be progressively eroded by natural science models. One version of this disciplinary imperialism propagated by some cognitive scientists is that religion itself is written into the psyche, maybe as a feature favouring selection. This seems to me contrary to empirical observation of secularisation in Europe. Religion in the former East Germany is of scant account and continues to decline, and with the demise of communism there are no plausible functional alternatives to fill the vacancy and to bolster the contention that religion arises naturally, in spite of the eager arguments of the Catholic philosopher Roger Trigg.[9] What matters for the present argument is the *difference* between what is written in and what is subject to transformation. I could translate that difference in theological language. The Gospel saying, 'It needs be that the offences will come', on account of sin,

---

9   Roger Trigg, 'Freedom, Toleration and the Naturalness of Religion' in S. Clarke, R. Powell and J. Savelescu (eds), *Religion, Intolerance and Conflict*, Oxford: Oxford University Press, 2012.

especially wars and rumours of wars, and the continuing existence of 'the poor' codes what must be. The demand for repentance and reformation, what the New Testament calls *metanoia*, codes what might be if we chose. What I said earlier about realism is also relevant here. Augustine of Hippo was a realist and his emphasis on the realities of social organisation contrasts with the emphasis of Pelagius on what may be changed by human volition and intervention. Augustine corresponds to one type of sociologist, Pelagius corresponds to another. That is why in the 1960s I somewhere described sociology as 'the documentation of original sin by those who believe in original virtue'.

I can now compare the obvious threat posed by the natural science model to theology with the more subtle threat posed by sociology. I shall then consider how sociology and theology both take off from the concept of self-transcendence and how they differ in the way they construe the difference between the real or the given, and what can be transcended or transformed. The issue of the embrace or rejection of violence provides a particularly illuminating marker for determining the degree of acceptance or rejection of 'the world' as dominated by 'the principalities and powers', and for determining the Christian angle of transcendence. I mean the degree of tension between the Christian vision and the realities of the human condition.

Finally I shall offer some instances of how this works out in exemplary instances when the visionary encounters the real and the given. As indicated in my initial introduction I appeal to Peter Brown's *Through the Eye of a Needle*[10] to show how the vision of the rule of God in the New Testament about the danger of riches is inflected by the realities of social organisation during the first six centuries of the Christian era. The issue of wealth provides another illuminating marker to place alongside the issue of violence for determining the angle of transcendence and the degree of tension. My second and third examples show how the rift between the visionary and the real, or in theological terms, between the rule of God and 'the powers' of this world, above all wealth, power and warfare, were experienced in the life of the twentieth-century musician Benjamin Britten, and by the seventeenth-century poet and parish priest George Herbert.

The example of Benjamin Britten as a passionate pacifist and a composer, dedicated to peaceful creation rather than to destructive warfare, will enable me to track another source of tension rooted simultaneously in the moral and the aesthetic. The example of George Herbert, in particular some of the most famous poems in his collection *The Temple*, will enable me to point to the Eucharist

---

[10]   Peter Brown, *Through the Eye of a Needle: Wealth, the Fall of Rome, and the Making of Christianity in the West, 350–550 AD*, Princeton: Princeton University Press, 2012.

as the love feast of table fellowship and the divine presence. The love feast of table fellowship represents an eschatological vision of humanity reconciled and at peace. But, as indicated earlier, the history of the Eucharist shows us how this supreme institution of human fellowship and divine presence itself becomes what faith identifies as 'a sign of division'. The blood given for others becomes a source of bloodshed and division. As already suggested it is in the realm of the transcendent sign and the moment of communion that the rift in experience between the social realities of wealth, power and violence on the one side and the peaceable sharing of gifts enjoined at the Last Supper on the other side is healed. The Eucharist enacts and literally embodies what Sarah Beckwith calls 'the grammar of forgiveness'.[11]

When people think of the conflict between science and religion, whether politicians, intellectuals or average citizens, they are thinking of the natural sciences not the cultural and hermeneutic disciplines.[12] The birth of the universe and the origin of species are not remotely like the opening verses of Genesis, angels are pious fictions, miracles do not happen and if they did would disrupt the ordered relations between phenomena on which both science and everyday practical activity depend. Virgins do not give birth and the dead do not rise again. Darwin finished off what Copernicus began. Some might throw in Freud on the future of illusions, and ideas about religion as immature projections of compensatory fantasies onto an uncaring universe. Even our vaunted altruism is so much self-replication in disguise devised by the cunning of 'the selfish gene'.

The sceptics do not have sociology in mind or even history, though they may suspect the Bible is not exactly history as we understand it, partly because it witnesses to events that the natural sciences show to be very unlikely. The idea that the Bible consists of the ill-informed speculations of goatherds and the deranged imaginations of shepherds, or represents incoherent relics of our superstitious past, rests on a conception of religious affirmations as failed propositions – a conception that owes everything to the model of natural science.

Here we encounter a crucial paradox. Sociology may not figure in the imagination of people who believe religion has been disproved by science, but for those who undergo professional formation as sociologists the subject appears

---

[11] Sarah Beckwith, *Shakespeare and the Grammar of Forgiveness*, Ithaca and London: Cornell University Press, 2011.

[12] Quintessentially they are thinking of the initial clash, in part a corrupt bureaucratic cock up, between a Christianity still largely attached to Aristotelian models and the Copernican revolution worked out and furthered by Galileo Galilei. This is covered in the discussion of religion and science in William Shea and Mark Davie (trans.), *Galileo: Selected Writings*, Oxford: Oxford University Press, 2012.

to subvert faith very effectively. Partly that is because it provides an initiation into the vast diversity of human social arrangements and contextualises the legitimations, the cosmologies and the notions of right and wrong that go with those arrangements. What we take for granted, especially what we elevate as natural rather than unnatural and perverse, is rendered precarious and provisional. Sociology makes us chronically afraid to describe anything as unnatural. The question of what is natural is not discussed in this essay, in part because it involves the infinitely convoluted relation of sex to violence and power, and the way in which an acute angle of transcendence generates reservations about sexuality, whether derived from Christianity itself or from Platonic and 'eastern' sources. One can at least be certain that a discussion carried out in polarised terms contrasting innocent natural instinct and repressive penitential regimens is totally inadequate. Sociology as practised is so much the discipline of surfaces that it has no handle on the often mutually reinforcing suctions represented by the arenas of social life identified by Weber as all, in one way or another, sites of tension between 'the world' and a given angle of transcendence. The nexus of sex and violence, representing the arenas of the erotic and the political, exemplifies what we now call extreme behaviour, though historically it is rather frequent. Somehow sociology has handed over to psycho-pathology large tracts of its own core concerns. One obvious contemporary instance is the relation between the eschatological violence of beheadings and crucifixions and the sexual slavery of women as currently practised by the so-called Islamic State. The Taiping Rebellion provides another instance. The alternative to total control is total antinomian licence.

Apart from destabilising all notions of what is natural, sociology, understood as in its inception part of the modernising project, analyses religion itself in terms of solidarity and conflict, and in terms of legitimations of power and human projections of alternative worlds. It also expropriates the impulse to love one's neighbour in order to achieve a rational reordering of society through impersonal bureaucratic administration. Sociology predicts the progressive displacement of religion by ideology, the confinement of faith to the irrational imaginations of the private sphere, and reduces religious concepts to reflections of more real forces. Sociology expropriates the social space occupied by religion. I believe that these expropriations postulated by sociology are projects masquerading as facts but their factual status is widely taken for granted.

I am saying that sociology is liable to undermine faith more effectively than most other subjects *and* that its practice brings it very close to theology in significant ways. I shall now try to explain. Theology codes the actual and the visionary, and so does sociology. But whereas sociology abstracts and generalises, theology exemplifies, dramatises, narrates, particularises and deals in condensed signs or symbols. Sociology may relegate theology to an outmoded stage of *explanation* understood as propositional hypotheses of the if-then variety, but theology remains *alongside* sociology as a profound mode of *understanding*. The old is not replaced by the new. Instead, truths are enriched and falsehoods and delusions are winnowed out. Imaginative understanding is not replaced by controlled explanation, and concrete myth and narrative are not replaced by abstract reason. Imaginative understanding, myth and narrative are always with us. They suffuse all our social life, political and personal, and not just the private sphere. As I have put it elsewhere, there is no *logos* without *mythos*.[13] In a similar way Robert Cover claims in his *Nomos and Narrative* that there is no *nomos* without narrative.[14] Norms are not so much thrown up intellectually as written in blood and carried by autonomous interpretive communities that either turn away from the state or attempt to capture it redemptively – and in so doing find their redemptive power partly confiscated or deflected.

Theology and sociology have this above all in common: they contemplate the gap between the real and the ideal and propose a practice that might bring them into closer alignment. They both exemplify at least three fundamental approaches. There is a realist approach stressing what must be and will be, that I trace back to Augustine. There is a meliorative approach based on pragmatic wisdom, prudence and what a Lutheran would call '*gut Regiment*' that goes back to the ancient Wisdom tradition and notions of decent civility. Finally there is a transformative or visionary approach that goes back to the Gospels and the hope of *metanoia*, and to some aspects of Judaism, notably Second Isaiah poised between the bitter experience of exile and the hope of a return to the homeland. I assume that the Hebrew Bible itself, the Tanakh, derives from that experience, though formalised in canonical form centuries later.

I now have to work out my implied programme by looking first at the history of religion, then at sociology, and finally at my specific examples that show how in the history of civilisations influenced by Christianity we shift to and fro between a stark recognition of the way the world is and more or less conforming to it or even relishing it, and envisaging a world restored, redeemed and at peace. Christianity runs 'against the grain', given that the grain is roughly as Machiavelli conceived it and as contemporary cognitive science articulates it. So there is nothing surprising about religions, and ideologies like nationalism,

---

[13]   David Martin, *Religion and Power: No Logos without Mythos*, Farnham: Ashgate, 2014.
[14]   Robert Cover, 'Nomos and Narrative', *Harvard Law Review*, 97(4) (1983): 4–16.

communism and fascism, that code the dynamics of solidarity and violence against the outsider and 'the Other'. What has to be explained is the emergence, especially over the last three thousand years that make up what Karl Jaspers called the Axial Age, of alternative codings of how 'the kingdom' might come on earth as it is in heaven. Christianity runs counter to our natural instincts and affections.

When we enquire into theology we ask exactly how and to what extent it runs counter to the ways of the world, and we need not distinguish too sharply between theology and actually existing Christianity, or actually existing Buddhism or whatever. We are looking for angles of transcendence and degrees of tension with 'the world' that in the course of the last three thousand years have generated the fundamental contrast between the ways of faith and the ways of the world, or, in other terms, between the ideal and the real, between what ought to be and what is. Religion no longer codes and sacralises the forces of nature and the powers that dominate society, but projects upward (or discovers and uncovers) nature and society as they ought to be. That is one major reason why we cannot talk in general about what some dubious entity called 'religion' does or does not characteristically do. Let me put it schematically for developments in the ancient Middle East. The king or pharaoh as shepherd of his people fails to deliver justice or prosperity or security, and people project a king of kings who rules over all the earth and who really does have the almighty power to deliver justice, prosperity and security. Earthly powers and the powers of nature and society are potentially de-sacralised.

This is the crucial secularisation that started three millennia ago, that was partly reversed by Catholicism, and is far from complete even now. Once a king of kings, who is understood as universal, compassionate and just, has been projected upwards onto the heavens, he too is tried and tested by experience, as were the divine kings of the ancient Middle East. People discover the problem of suffering and injustice. That discovery animates the Psalms understood as poems of trust in 'the Lord' as king, that alternate faith in his immediate or eventual presence with protest at his absence, indifference and failure to protect. When 'the people of God' are frustrated with the present they throw the ideal kingdom into the future and the past. This puts pressure on time understood as a preparation for a transformation or for a first and a second advent. That pressure generates an oscillation between divine re-creation and/or redemption, and attempts to set up the kingdom by violence, as in Münster, the English Civil War and the revolutionary events of 1792 and 1917.

This oscillation is present in the Gospels themselves (as well as in a wider social context that includes the Zealots and some violent millenarian expectation), though whether its sources lie in the Evangelists or the disciples, or Christ himself, cannot be determined. There is a shadowy but unmistakeable violent alternative within the Gospels focused on Davidic kingship and the political restoration of Israel. This alternative persists alongside the emphasis on service rather than the exercise of power (as practised among the Gentiles), on the inwardness of the kingdom rather than the onset of immediate coercive power, and on turning the other cheek rather than retaliation or the threat of imminent eschatological destruction for those who fail to understand or respond. There are two cruces in the Gospel narratives that can be regarded as oscillating ambiguously in alternative directions: the four verses in Luke (22:35-8) where the disciples are seemingly encouraged to recognise a change of direction signified by the suggestion they buy swords, and the triumphant Davidic entry into Jerusalem, even though it takes places on a humble donkey. I think the weight of evidence lies with the non-violent understanding of the Gospels stated unequivocally in the response of Jesus before Pilate: 'My kingdom is not of this world, else would my servants fight.'

The kingdom 'cometh not by observation', according to the Gospels, but suffers violence and lies in wait.[15] In the Christian narrative the servant king proclaims the rule of righteousness, peace and plenitude through anticipatory signs. He provokes a confrontation with 'the world' in which he takes on himself the burden and the cost of sin and death, and redeems and triumphs over it through a demonstration of love, forgiveness and strength through weakness. He overcomes the world, not by power but by entering into the world to show how the lost might be brought back to life through the fires of judgement and love. At any rate these are the phrases that theology devises to render account of the atonement, but maybe one needs also to say that the cross is the way it happened, a contingency in prospect rendered necessary in retrospect.

That is the shortest possible schematisation of a long transition in the ancient Near East, notably the region between the Euphrates and the Nile, that carries forward and combines with all kinds of earlier material, for example the war-god and the thunder-god or residual manifestations of the querulous and tyrannical non-entity William Blake calls 'Old Nobodaddy',[16] and councils of the gods under a president of the immortals. However, there are other negotiations between the real and the ideal over the last three thousand years in other regions, notably India, China and Greece, which turn on different angles of transcendence and

---

[15] Luke 17:20.

[16] Blake uses the term frequently to refer to punitive gods, including in the early poem 'To Nobodaddy', in David V. Erdman (ed.), *The Complete Poetry and Prose of William Blake*, New York: Anchor, 1965, p. 471.

different degrees of tension. Where the angle of transcendence is acute the likely result is monasticism, as in Buddhism; where it is modest as in China, the likely result is the figure of the sage; where it both judges the world and accepts it as in principle good, the likely result is a split along the lines set out by Ernst Troeltsch between a compromising church and monastic virtuosi inside the church and sects and prophets protesting from culturally recognised outposts on the outside. Here we have the Weberian contrast between prophet and priest to set alongside Troeltsch's contrast between church and sect.

If we focus on Christianity as one major realisation of potentials in Judaism, notably the spiritualisation of the local terrestrial city as the universal heavenly city, or of the exile and the homeland as universal conditions of the human soul, or the shift away from external ritual and statute to inward grace and faith, the specific angle of transcendence generates a symbolic logic or a thematic repertoire. Theology seeks to render this symbolic logic in what one might call 'The Great Code', following William Blake, whether in compromising church or in radical sect and utopian community. Theology, then, is an '-ology' like sociology and all the other '-ologies', but its mode of operation has characteristics already hinted at. These are best illustrated by offering examples of what I mean by its symbolic logic and its characteristic transformations. Theology is a generative grammar derived from a limited set of fundamental presuppositions representing different angles of transcendence.

How does the thematic repertoire play out in the case of Christianity? Here I am well aware that I offer an idealisation for what is emergent by degrees in the Gospels and embedded in the status of Jesus as a Jew addressing first his own people. First of all let me take the double entendre created by the angle of transcendence between the givens of existence, the raw data or 'capta' of the human condition, and the visionary transformation or revelation. This double entendre allows condensed signs like city and desert to be overheard in two registers, physical and spiritual, and it becomes aligned with the contrast between the real and the visionary in regulatory ideas like the two kingdoms, the two swords and the two cities, and the contrast of Nature and Grace. There is a spiritual brotherhood constituted by the free gift of blood, and another blood brotherhood of arms that lives by shedding blood. The brotherhood of arms is part of the physical dynamic of attack and defence, and it is shadowed, as Jessica Martin remarks, by a clear movement in Scripture from the bloodthirsty divinity who demands the expulsion of the Other from promised lands, to the divinity who is expelled 'out of the land of the living' to become the blood donor to anyone open to receive the gift.[17] The border that separates those who adhere to the ethnic community, ideally united with a capital city and a territory, and signalled by circumcision, is transferred to a border created by commitment to travelling though darkness to light, and through death to life and resurrection in the waters of baptism. The physical Jordan, understood as a crossing place into a promised land, becomes an image and an enactment of a transition. The river has become a baptismal rite of transformation or *metanoia* which is symbolically transferred to children as part of their acceptance into 'the people of God'. Sacraments are colonies of grace implanted in the world of nature.

Once an increased angle of transcendence has dramatised the contrast between obvious reality and a universal vision of redemption or restoration, time becomes urgent with the need to choose. People are visited with a sense of desolation and anticipation, of the promise of the kingdom and the fear of destruction, of being reunited with the Father of all in loving communion and being orphaned, of being under the threat of malign powers and being assured of ultimate victory. This thematic repertoire is not a set of fantasies confined to a paranoid and oppressed minority, though it certainly can be that, but constitutive of whole civilisations in which its seeds are deposited and propagated.

The symbolic logic works itself out through signs of a kingdom already present, for example, in Jesus' distribution of food to thousands gathered at the lakeside, or the changing of water to wine at the wedding feast. It shows itself in all the imagery of seeds secretly germinating under the surface and in the anticipated reversal in 'the kingdom' of the worldly evaluations of people and things. That reversal turns on the contrast between the flowers of the field and 'Solomon in all his glory', and the contrast between the consciously righteous and sinners whose readiness to respond gives them precedence in the 'age to come'. The expectation of a transition is coded in the baptismal image of descending into death to ascend into life that also provides the pattern of the creed: 'when I fall I rise', 'the one that descended is also the one who ascended', the Lord is the suffering servant and the suffering servant is the Lord. Each moment of epiphany or communion is attended by mortal danger: the newborn holy child is threatened by mass murder and the communion of the brotherhood at the last supper is threatened by treason and denial. Everything is literally precarious.

Theology works out this condensed sign language. It follows through its characteristic transformations, especially when faith as a practice encounters the realities of wealth and power, when the icons and images of the hoped-for transformation are partly expropriated by access of power and wealth, and

---

17   Personal communication.

when the autonomous interpretive communities flee from the corrupt and violent 'City of Man' to the solitary place or the segregated group or cell. As already indicated there are various intermediate positions, such as the attempt to create a good city, Philadelphia, informed by norms of civility, and aided by the resources of the Wisdom tradition.

All this may seem far from Weber on economic ethics and the vocation of politics, or Marx on expropriation, alienation and fetishism, or Durkheim on the ways in which our solidarities and conflicts are projected and symbolised in our totems and taboos. But my examples do not seek to dramatise the difference between a social science and theology, so much as to hint at their similarity and their occupation of much the same space. I have already indicated my disagreement with what for me are deformed and positivist versions of social science that reject the perspectives of the classics, and of the critical forms of sociology, as well as ignoring the phenomenological approach to sociology and theology as monitoring the contours and interior movement of religious experience.

The world of nature and the social world, especially in its political aspect, is obviously based on conflict as well as cooperation, on violence as well as nurture, on the One both with and against the Other, but 'the obvious' is only made explicit by a Darwin or a Machiavelli. Similar considerations apply to another realist, Georges Sorel, in his classic of political science, *Reflections on Violence*.[18] Sorel showed that politics and religion alike are realms of overarching mythic narratives and images that mobilise groups for action. It ought always to have been obvious that politics and religions occupy similar space and that myth lies at the heart of political action.

Sociologists and political scientists, in common with theologians, are divided into realists (or pessimists), meliorists and visionaries. Niccolò Machiavelli and Georges Sorel are realists. Max Weber was pessimistic about the consequences of rational bureaucracy, and Tönnies was pessimistic about the decline of *Gemeinschaft*, while there is a whole sociological tradition that notes and laments the decline of community in modernity. John Gray is a dystopian who treats humans as 'straw dogs' and regards the Enlightenment illusion of the triumph of reason as parasitic on Christianity.[19] Postmodernist thinkers enjoy delusion in a spirit of irony where all the actors play a game of insubstantial masks. Talcott Parsons was a meliorist anticipating convergence. Rousseau was

---

18   Georges Sorel, *Reflections on Violence*, Cambridge: Cambridge University Press, 1999.
19   John Gray, *Black Mass: Apocalyptic Religion and the Death of Utopia*, New York: Penguin Books, 2007.

a visionary in laying the foundations of a whole school of educational sociology based on the premise that man was born free but everywhere bound in the chains of culture. The debates in education and criminology alike are informed by assumptions about what is unavoidable and what is transformable. These are the nubs of contention.

Apart from its purely experimental forms, psychology also reflects fundamental assumptions about the real that cannot be avoided and potentials for transformation. Formulations of stages of personal 'growth' are as much normative as analytic. Studies of prejudice are riddled with pre-judgements based on values. Abraham Maslow's formulation of a hierarchy of needs was clearly inflected by values as well as facts. Freudianism, understood as myth masquerading as science, exists in realist forms stressing the inevitable costs of civilisation and the need for suppression, and other forms stressing the therapeutic value of free expression. Notions of cultural authenticity and distinctions between a false self and a true or authentic self and concepts like anomie and alienation suggest the extent to which practitioners of the social sciences and theology tread similar territory.

Concluding Examples

My first concluding example is Peter Brown's *Through the Eye of a Needle*.[20] Brown analyses how the visionary perspective of Christianity concerning wealth and riches encounters the realities of the social order, especially once the body of Christians includes some wealthy people in the late fourth century. Augustine is the key figure because his concept of the City of God and the City of Man codes the dilemma central to everything discussed so far: the chasm between a non-violent community where goods are shared, and enduring economic and political realities. The chasm can be negotiated in any number of ways but it cannot be bridged except in moments of communion and ecstasy of the kind experienced by Pascal, or (rather differently) by the contemplative prayer practised by Teresa of Avila. Pelagius is also important because he believes human initiative can successfully negotiate the tension between the Gospel and 'the world'. Augustine and Pelagius correspond to different kinds of sociology: Augustine is a realist recognising the depredations of sin and the recalcitrance of 'the world' and Pelagius a meliorist who finds 'the world', including humanity, more amenable to natural human goodwill. Augustine recognises that the very

---

[20]   Brown, *Through the Eye of a Needle*.

imperfect institutions of the political and economic order are interim bulwarks against the ultimate threat of anarchy and 'the war of all against all'.

One option for Christians is to maintain the tension. Or one might conceive of a two-tier Church, where the laity engaged in good works and monks gave up their possessions to live a life in common. Another option is simply to recommend that Christians go beyond conventional displays of charity to the citizenry to include 'the poor'. Sometimes that might mean giving through the clergy or to the clergy, especially the monks, so that the Church itself became a repository of corporate wealth. Paulinus of Nola endowed a shrine of which he became the patron. By the sixth century the rich were often inclined to deploy their wealth at the end of their lives to buy paradise by endowing the church in return for its prayers. The radicalism of the Gospel had been subverted to the point where the wealthy could buy paradise and the poor could not. As usual radicalism trails unintended consequences: the rest is the history of Tetzel and the Reformation.

In 1913 Benjamin Britten was born into a semi-secular society about to destroy itself through war, violence and economic collapse. Without being a convinced believer, he was attracted to a radical Christian vision and he fused it with a radical political vision. This fusion found expression in a passionate pacifism uniting social concern with a repudiation of the capitalist order. As war approached he joined the pacifist protest, with its unstable mixture of political and religious motifs, and then left England for America with the poet W.H. Auden. In his rejection of violence Britten appealed to the imperative of creativity as well as morality. In other words the rift between real and visionary, as understood in Weberian terms of religious rejections of the world, runs not only through the whole gamut of the economic and political order, including violence, but extends to the aesthetic. Britten rejected the obligation to fight specifically as a creator and artist.

Britten oscillated between exploration of the harshness of the world and intimations of transcendence. His operatic heroes are either flawed outsiders or innocents destroyed by corrupt power, by the necessary operations of the law and the search for scapegoats. Some of Britten's church works frame the depredations of sin with moments of reconciliation, often against the backdrop of the choreography of liturgy, as in the Church Parable *Curlew River*. It is the disposition of bodies in liturgical choreography and gesture, rather than what Auden in his 'Anthem for Saint Cecilia's Day' dismissed as 'outworn images' and 'ruined languages', that complement the power of music to achieve intimations of restoration and redemption.[21] Britten is a major representative of a shift in modernist poetry back to the liturgical that is also found (staying with English examples) in Eliot, Auden and David Jones. Nevertheless, Britten never directly confronts the tension between the contradictory visions of the real and what may be hoped for. He shudders away from the real, as we all do, so that after visiting Belsen he tried to frame the raw violence of his *The Rape of Lucretia* with an unintegrated commentary appealing to Christian forgiveness and redemption. The terrible political violence of the concentration camp and the exemplary interpersonal violence of rape could not be glossed by generalised appeals to forgiveness that did not face the costs entailed for all the participants in any full redemption. Britten evaded the cost by staying within the aesthetic reconciliation.

George Herbert was born in 1593. He was one of a group of metaphysical poets and writers, often influenced by Neoplatonism, who celebrated what another metaphysical, Henry Vaughan, called 'the great chime and symphony of Nature',[22] and the Christian narrative of redemption. Here is another premature harmonisation of the chasm in experience between Nature understood as 'the great chime' and what was later described by Tennyson in Darwinian terms as 'Nature red in tooth and claw'.[23] Most of these metaphysical poets bridged the rift between the real and the visionary through music: hence the potent analogy of 'chime' and 'harmony'. It is interesting that this was the Age of Discovery and the Puritan Revolution, and these writers were influenced by the scientific revolution, in Herbert's case through Francis Bacon and his epoch-making *The Advancement of Learning* of 1605 where he inaugurated a programme of inductive natural science that replaced words by facts and numbers.

Herbert looked on Nature and humanity alike as a harmonious creation, where each element manifested a character tending towards God. 'The obvious' truth about inveterate conflict was obscured in favour of reconciliation. However, Herbert faced a different conflict between a secular career based on the usual scramble for place, power and privilege, and a priestly life of love and prayer.[24] His third poem on love concerns the invitation from a great Lord to sit at his table and 'share his meat'. Here it is love that reconciles as well as music.

[21] W.H. Auden, section 3 of 'Anthem for St. Cecilia's Day' (for Benjamin Britten), in *Collected Shorter Poems 1927–1957*, London: Faber, 1966, p. 175.
[22] Henry Vaughan, 'The Morning Watch', in *Silex Scintillans* (1650), London: Scolar Press, 1970.
[23] Alfred, Lord Tennyson, *In Memoriam*, in *Selected Poems*, London: Penguin, 2007.
[24] John Drury, *Music at Midnight: The Life and Poetry of George Herbert*, London: Penguin, 2013.

The guest is hesitant because unworthy and needs assurance from the host before he can partake of the feast: Herbert writes 'Love bade me welcome but my soul drew back guilty of dust and sin'. The poem concludes when the host says that he has borne the cost of sin so his guest need have no fear. He is covered by grace. 'So I did sit and eat.' Love has crossed the chasm and broken every barrier down. The cost has been paid.

Herbert's poem has had an extensive afterlife, and its influence on Simone Weil illustrates a rift within the soul of an extraordinary woman racked by the gap between the Christian vision and her terrible experience of the realities of industrial society. It greatly influenced Weil during her many sufferings, particularly when she shared the conditions of workers at the Renault factory. She manifested in her own frail body the most exacting tension between radical Christian and radical political visions and economic and political realities. She was abused by her comrades on the left for telling the truth about the Soviet Union. She rejected French scepticism as having nothing to offer and yet felt able only to stand in the threshold of the Church. Nevertheless she went briefly to the monastery of Solemnes and was introduced by an English Catholic woman to the seventeenth-century metaphysical poets. It was Herbert's poem on love, repeated with the Lord's Prayer, especially during the enactment of the liturgy and the music of plainsong, that made it possible for her to be possessed by the divine presence in a world that seemed to testify to the gap between Christianity and 'the grain of the universe'. The gap between real conflict and ideal peace was closed for her in a moment of transcendence by the evocative power of beauty and the gestures of reconciliation in the liturgy.

First Commentary

On Sin and Primal Violence; on the Language of Atonement and the Restoration of Fellowship in the Resurrection; on Time as the Generator of Meaning, Action and Motive; on Divinity Revealed in the Human Face

We begin with primal violence as the critical marker of the ways of an unredeemed world and of the distance between Christianity and 'the grain' of that world. Anthropologists have recently unearthed a skull roughly dated from well over 400,000 years ago that provides evidence of violence between humans. The story of Cain and Abel is a mythical representation of primal violence and it reminds us that violence is often the consequence of fraternal rivalry. Those united by blood turn on each other in bloody rivalry. Warriors band together in fictive ties of blood brotherhood to shed the blood of their rivals and secure the scarce 'goods' that generate their rivalry. And scarcity never ends, even when we can satisfy our immediate needs: desire comprises an ever-expanding universe.

Of course, power is the source of order as well as of internecine disorder. Nothing can be achieved without order and those who represent that order will characteristically strain every sinew to protect it from the threat of anarchy and what Thomas Hobbes called the 'war of all against all' whereby everyone lives according to a regime where the success of one group or individual is achieved at the expense of another. Settled order is precarious and precious. It will often be the consequence of sedimented violence practised on subordinate populations over generations until it acquires apparent solidity and even legitimacy. Those in power will act swiftly against anyone who challenges that legitimacy. They will rapidly seek to eliminate anyone or any group plausibly defined as disturbing the peace and ask questions later. To the degree that power is unstable, the maintenance of order becomes of primary concern not the requirements of justice. Inevitably justice has its uses: blatant injustice can undermine the imperative of power and judicious clemency can enhance it. But clemency exercised at the risk of loss of authority and interpreted as a sign of weakness is the prelude to disaster.

Power is averse to risk and under pressure its demands are likely to outweigh the requirements of justice. Just as violence is inherent in the human situation so is injustice. The axe does not fall on the head of malefactors but falls on evil-doers and the innocent alike in response to the imperatives of successful domination. This is what is meant by terror: the willingness of those contending for domination to do whatever it takes to achieve their ends, with the proviso that terror is not counter-productive. Terror represents the raw logic of successful power and the negative dynamic of the imperative of survival. Under the universal pressure of scarcity humankind turns murderous. Brother's hand is raised against brother and we return to the primal myth with which we began.

What is unique in human history is an angle of transcendence in Christianity and Buddhism that rejects this universal logic of power through a resolute refusal to co-operate with the necessities of violence and with the cycles of malign reciprocity based on honour codes associated with those necessities. It does so by advertising what these cycles of malign reciprocity entail through a refusal to overcome evil with good. As the Sermon on the Mount puts it: 'Resist not him that is evil, but overcome evil with good.' By adopting the posture of powerlessness and accepting the dire costs of defencelessness Christianity presents to 'the world' a tableau of 'the kingdom'. Integrity confronts political expediency. But this is not a way through the political problem. It does not dispense with the need for politics or the negotiated settlements between rival sources of power that are so conspicuously absent from the Gospels. The Gospels focus on the temptations of power but they are in no way sources of political prescription or the management of disputes and competing claims, and for that we must be grateful, else we would be saddled with settled answers where no such answers exist.

No state can ignore the dynamic of negative reciprocity and of politic pre-emption and survive. 'The world' is constituted quite otherwise and to attempt to build policy on the principled rejection of violence and domination is to court the universal disaster of anarchy where 'no man can work'. What Christianity achieves presents to the moral imagination precisely what the world order entails. It exposes its true nature and our true nature for all to see. 'Behold and see if there be any sorrow like unto my sorrow.' Moreover, the human spectators of the dereliction of the Man of Sorrows, impaled on 'the tree' at Golgotha, share in those sorrows. Like the sufferers from the plague in the Antonine monastery in Colmar they read in the sufferings of Christ the divine identification with their plight. These sufferings are presented as the consequences of sin and the regime of unrighteousness.

However, is that really the case? Here we encounter a major problem to which we must return because only some suffering arises as the consequence of sin and a regime of unrighteousness. There are other kinds of suffering, notably sickness and death itself, that are not due to such a regime. St Paul attributes the suffering of humanity to the sin of Adam and that in turn implies that sickness has a direct relation to sin. But that solution is morally intolerable and specifically denied by Jesus in his negative response in St John's Gospel 9:3 to a question about whether the sufferings of a blind man were due to his own sin or to the sin of his parents. If that were indeed the case that would imply that disablement, for example, derives from moral fault and not from natural scientific causation. The wider context of this is the Jewish and, at certain periods, Christian belief that wholeness of body and soul go together. The consequences of this were very wide-ranging and they have required a moral revolution to reverse. That is presumably why 'no feeble person' (Psalm 105:37) was found among the Jews who made their escape from Egypt.

So we have two great chains of causation, one moral to be understood in the perspective of the social sciences, and the other natural to be dealt with by the natural sciences. Paul's attribution of natural death and physical suffering as conditions to be understood as 'caused' by sin wrongly treats them as part of the great chain of moral causation. This could make perfectly good sense were he referring to spiritual death, because spiritual death is a moral condition. But he appears to be placing spiritual and natural death under the same rubric, an approach which has the unsustainable moral implications about sin, suffering and disablement already referred to. After all, his contrast between the work of the first Adam and the work of the second Adam in 1 Corinthians 15 turns on the antithesis of death and resurrection: *For since by man came death by man came also the resurrection of the dead.* I think we can assume that Paul is not treating resurrection as a spiritual condition only, so we can also assume that he has introduced a fundamental confusion between the great chain of moral causation and the great chain of natural causation. That means that we need a naturalistic account of moral causation without appeal to a supernatural plan overseen by God. I have already indicated such a naturalistic account in relation to the dynamics of politics as it is practised in 'the world'. I now need to amplify that account further.

The account I have given of the injustice that arises out of the necessities of politics can be further followed through in the context of political choices which are also profoundly interpersonal: the personal and the political are not easily disentangled. From the beginning of life until its ending human beings exist in networks of connection mediated by language where they act sometimes co-operatively, sometimes violently to secure access to scarce goods understood as objects of desire incompatible with each other and with the desires or needs of others. These goods are not themselves necessarily 'good' for those seeking after them but are persisted in because at any particular moment the short-term cost of relinquishing them appears to exceed the gain of being freed from the burdens they impose. People become bound by assumed obligations or pressures and by the residual allure of their initial desires and feel they have lost their ability to choose. They are entrapped by their own choices which are themselves the consequences of previous decisions.

The violence generated by the sense of entrapment is then visited elsewhere in a moral chain of injustice which may well spawn other chains of the same kind. One minor example of entrapment might be that the responsible person within a group fails to do justice once in case he is logically compelled to do it again. Alternatively, the one on whom the ultimate responsibility for decisions rests fears to exercise mercy where mercy is morally appropriate in case he imperils his own authority or erodes the moral authority of the rule that has been broken. Thus in Herman Melville's story of *Billy Bud*, which inspired Benjamin Britten's opera, the innocent suffers on account of the principle that 'It is expedient one die for the people'. The paradox of the story lies in the fact that Billy is guilty of violence because he struck his superior, Master of Arms, Mr Claggart, out of frustrated righteous indignation when Claggart set him up for an unjust charge of theft and treason. Billy is in this sense Everyman in that the 'innocent' is never wholly innocent since we are all implicated in chains of violence and injustice. The same is true of Captain Vere, the commander of the ship, who is ultimately responsible for order and good discipline under the pressure of wartime exigencies. Vere chooses not to exercise mercy after the officers have found Billy guilty and condemned him to hanging, and spends the rest of his life lamenting Billy's fate and his own unavoidable role in it. Captain Vere is trapped in moral necessities that entail his enactment of a judgement that cannot take account of Billy's purity of intention in spite of the nature and quality of his murderous act. The parallels with the Passion story are clearly intended, with Vere in the role of Pilate.

These perverse chains of moral causation mean that death and violence are endemic and that the relatively innocent regularly pay the highest costs. In the case of the Passion narrative the totally innocent pays the total cost, even to the extent of experiencing alienation from God and the ultimate dereliction of a break in communion. The one who seeks with integrity to fulfil the will of his Father enters into the abyss of desolation. There are two supremely redemptive moments in the Passion narrative: one where the redeemer experiences the consequences of sin through separation from God as the source of his being, and the other when he exculpates the agents of his undeserved suffering on the ground that they do not realise what they are doing. They are unwitting players in a cosmic drama far outstripping their conscious agency. We, as the spectators of this appalling scene, simultaneously acknowledge our profound implication in the chains of violence and injustice that have brought about the death of the innocent and recognise that this drama far exceeds in its horror anything we have consciously willed or desired. It has all led to *this*. We know that the burden of our collective transgressions has fallen upon him. We also know this spectacle dramatises the divine love towards his creatures in that God himself takes our death upon him in order to offer us his eternal life. He has reversed the meaning of death to re-enter it in the column of life.

We come here to the theme of the stone that was rejected and then is made the foundation stone and headstone. There are many images that speak of Christ as the stone and the rock, and other images that speak of the congregation of Christ's friends as living stones in an invisible temple in the heavenly Jerusalem. One reason for this is that the words 'stone' and 'son' are as close to each other in Hebrew as they are in English. The governing idea is that in Christ the scattered elements are once more gathered together and the ruins of our human estate restored. We are once more 'fitly joined together' because the body of Christ was and is broken on our account. We are made whole because he took upon him our brokenness and raised our humanity into God. So we have a ruin that is reassembled as a new temple, a descent into our condition which makes possible our ascent into God, and a brokenness which has been made whole. This is the great Christian drama of contrasted signs: good and evil, abased and exalted, descended and ascended, wounded and healed, broken and restored, fragmented and made whole, scattered and rejoined together. Christian language consists of these fundamental antitheses.

A further antithesis worth exploring, and one that illustrates how metaphors proliferate to all the sectors of experience, is that between rigidity and liberation, the bonds of slavery and the releasing tears of repentance that show the stony heart has melted. Peter Brown discusses this in relation to the way Bishop Gregory of Tours in the sixth century sees the miracles of the saints as prefigurations of the restoration of order in the forgiveness of sins at the Day of Judgement. Brown shows how medical models of bodily cure and theological models of forgiveness echo each other. He quotes from Gregory:

just as the saints here lance all kinds of illnesses here [*hic*], so they deflect the ruthless penalties of torment there [*illic*]; that just as they alleviate bodily fevers here, so they quench the eternal flames there; that just as they clear out the horrible ulcers of leprosy here, so through their intervention they obtain release from the blemishes of sins there.[1]

I have been trying in much of my discussion so far to give a naturalistic account of how the innocent suffers on account of the guilty in a chain of negative moral causation and to show how the search for atonement is generated by our alienation from the sources of our own good. We seek reconciliation in a restored communion. But communion is not fully restored without comprehensive recognition of what has happened. Confession and penitence as practised by Christians from the earliest centuries to the present recognise what has happened in general but they do not pursue this generic recognition to the point where the trail of damage is examined and exposed in detail. That is because the truth in such matters is too painful to everyone concerned and all too likely to postpone the closure that participants profoundly desired. Complete closure is very difficult to achieve.

The account is naturalistic in terms of the human situation in which we all find ourselves because the alternative account would have to postulate a divine plan based on a providential oversight over the nature and destiny of humankind for which there is no evidence whatever. Nor is the question of evidence for providential oversight the main point at issue. One could imagine such evidence by postulating a plan beyond our comprehension or a plan to be realised in a marvellous way yet to be revealed, and it would just be unfortunate that most of humankind suffered appallingly on the way to this ultimate epiphany. But such an imaginary solution based on the very long term is not morally sustainable any more than the Pauline attribution of suffering and death to sin is sustainable.

The main point at issue concerns human freedom and the moral problem of a creator who places his creature in an intolerable situation. As I have emphasised throughout this argument, we are dealing with two chains of causation that must not be confused. One is a moral chain of injustice built into human society though the complex operations of a regime of violence. The other 'plan' is well caught in the famous hymn by Mrs Cecil Alexander: 'There was no other good enough/to pay the price of sin/He only could unlock the gate/Of heaven and let us in.' It is also caught in a scheme of extraordinary intellectual and imaginative

---

[1]   Peter Brown, *The Ransom of the Soul: Afterlife and Wealth in Early Western Christianity*, Harvard and London: Harvard University Press, 2015, p. 176.

grandeur in Milton's *Paradise Lost* where the poet strives to 'justify the ways of God to man'. According to this plan God gave humans a freedom which they are more than likely to misuse and on account of this act of initial rebellion by the first Adam God condemned them in perpetuity to death and suffering and what Milton calls 'all our woe'. Adam rightly protests that God's response is totally disproportionate but, faced with overwhelming power, he submits to divine decree. It is worth noticing here that Milton in the course of the narrations attributed to Raphael in Book Eleven covers most of the bases explored in this book within the scope of the fundamental Pauline linkage of sin with death. According to Raphael's account of sacred history up to the time of the Deluge humankind gave ample evidence of the profound link between sex and violence. The deluge enables Noah to emerge as a typological prefiguring of Christ as the one righteous man. Raphael also indicates a source for the spiritual ambivalence of the aesthetic. Elsewhere in Milton it is clear that the angels sing harmoniously in celestial concerts before God 'in endless morn of light', but in Raphael's narration sweet harmony seduces humankind to sensuality.[2]

According to the 'plan', since God was the fount of justice someone had to pay the price of sin and reconcile man to God. The only one who could pay this price was his own dearly beloved son free of the taint of sin and therefore the one fit propitiation of his Father's offended majesty. Jesus became our high priest representing us before the throne of grace and averting the Father's just wrath against us on account of offended justice. By his death and resurrection Jesus overcame the bondage of sin and in principle restored us to communion with the Father and opened the gates of everlasting life to all who put their trust in his saving grace for justification. He offered God a *Full, perfect and sufficient sacrifice, oblation and satisfaction for the sins of the whole world*.[3]

Stated like that God is charged with setting up a 'scheme' of salvation where man is bound by the gift of freedom to commit the offences that attract the wrath of a just God. He is then condemned to punishment or at any rate to alienation from the source of his being apart from his acceptance of the grace of Christ. That grace saves him from condemnation: *There is therefore no condemnation to them that are in Christ Jesus*. This release on account of the love of God manifest in his son in order that we might be once more at one with him would be moving, and

---

[2] A profound Christian interpretation of Milton which does not justify the ways of God can be found in eight meditations by Jessica Martin, originally published in the *Guardian* in 2012 (see http://www.theguardian.com/commentisfree/belief/2011/nov/28/milton-paradise-lost-epic) and now available as an ebook: Jessica Martin, *John Milton: How to Believe*, Guardian Shorts, London: Guardian Books, 2013.

[3] *Book of Common Prayer*, Holy Communion.

indeed it is moving, were it not incarcerated in a morally unacceptable plan. The same is true of the sentence that summarises the atonement in a sublime moment in Handel's *Messiah*: 'And the Lord hath laid on him the iniquity of us all.' It has to be released from the context of God's planned intention and heard as saying that our iniquity has in the intricate course of moral causation fallen upon the head of Christ. It is important to retain access to some very powerful language while disburdening it of morally dubious associations with the theory of penal substitution. The language has to be lifted out of the context of the so-called plan.

The idea of a divine plan and an all-pervading Providence indicts God in the most serious way as the supposed 'planner' and we need to show why that is the case. Take, for example, the idea expressed in one of Bach's greatest cantatas that God's time, and specifically with regard to the hour of our death, is the best time: *Gottes Zeit ist die allerbeste Zeit*. This implies that God micro-manages all our times and seasons and is responsible for whatever befalls us. Now the time of death is an event within the great chain of natural causation and if God condemns some to die and others to live he is morally responsible for the obvious and massive injustices involved. The elderly person renders thanks for a presumed divine reprieve from cancer and at the same time the mother mourns her son struck down by cancer. Naturally this can stimulate the question 'what have I done to deserve this?' as if the world is manipulated by the divine planner according to some moral scheme. But that is very clearly not the case and in the case of illness a purely natural scientific sequence is treated as a sequence informed, however inexplicably, by moral criteria. People pray about their situation as though inserting an additional variable into a mix presided over by a slightly absent-minded deity in need of reminders. They also take comfort in supposing it is all in God's hands in the sense that he has their personal good at heart when the changes and chances of this fleeting world give one no encouragement to suppose this is the case. They say piously that all is as God wills when he bears no such responsibility. Prayer has to be for strength to encounter anxiety and loss, not to take upon oneself co-responsibility with the divine planner for whatever may befall.

The same notion of a divine planner suffuses the politics of the Old Testament and again it morally indicts God. Israel is comforted with the supposition that righteousness attracts divine favour and warned that unrighteousness attracts adverse political judgement and disaster. According to this account of divine Providence, whole empires rise and decay in relation to the special care exercised by God with regard to the survival of Israel. The Egyptians, the Assyrians, the Babylonians and the Persians are manipulated by God specifically with the moral and physical condition of a small group on the eastern littoral of the

Mediterranean especially in mind. Again, the moral implications of this view of history are intolerable. One might further conclude, as many have done, that historical success is a sign of divine favour, in which case some very surprising candidates for divine favour have come out on top while some very deserving candidates have been defeated or wiped out.

The problems of a providential view of history are not confined to the Hebrew Scriptures. Christians regularly repeat promises made in what is for them the Old Testament about a future kingdom here on earth. For example, it is supposed that God will set up a kingdom reigned over by Christ that has no end because he has put all his enemies under his feet. Christmas lessons promise that the increase of his government will have no end. This material version of the kingdom is very unattractive, especially as it seems to mirror the fear instilled by the ultimate servile state. One needs only look at the words of hymns unthinkingly sung by Christian congregations to gauge their political implications were they taken literally. Charles Wesley's fine hymn 'Rejoice the Lord is King' speaks of the people of God triumphing evermore as they are transported beyond the confines of this earthly realm.

As with other imagery, the anticipations of the kingdom belong to the space between longing and attainment. The kingdom of God is a secret growth fructifying in our lives and imaginations. It belongs to those reborn in the *spirit*, as Jesus said to Nicodemus when he came to visit the Lord by night. Again, as Jesus said to an enquirer in Mark 12:34, 'Thou are not far from the kingdom.' John Wesley pointed out in a sermon that the kingdom 'is not meat and drink', though imaginatively it is feasting together in shared table fellowship. Solidified, the kingdom would be an intolerable oriental despotism. Indeed that was precisely how many early Christians imagined divine government: petitioners sought clemency from the judgement of God as they sought clemency from the emperor.

It is worth saying again that there is no plausible evidence that God has intentions for his creatures that one day could justify the immense tally of human suffering. The plan is morally unsustainable. As already argued, the wrath of God appears totally out of proportion to the sin that man by his nature is bound to commit. The natural sufferings and death that he supposedly 'deserves' on account of sin are wildly disproportionate and the result of a confusion of moral causation with natural causation. This is not to say that actions and moral choices do not entail natural consequences. They do, and the natural consequence may be very serious. If we assume that obesity is in some cases a matter of cumulative choices over time the consequence may be death. The consequences of promiscuity may likewise be death. Work is necessary to each and every kind of achievement but pursued at the expense of body and soul it spreads destruction and death far and wide. But these consequences are not punishments devised by a wrathful deity any more than ebola is a consequence of divine judgement on account of sin. It is those same energies that power life that can turn deadly. There is often hell to pay for our actions in terms of damage to ourselves and others, but the hell is of our own and not divine devising.

How then might we restate in summary form an acceptable doctrine of atonement? The atonement attempts to unite in the bond of peace what had been divided, and to reconcile the alienated. It seeks to cross the chasm between the kingdom of peace and righteousness as proclaimed with anticipatory signs in the Gospels, and the violence of the world. It does so by absorbing the violence in the body of the redeemer. The redeemer absorbs into himself the impact of the regime of violence and conflict. He 'takes it upon him'. We read the realities of domination, power and expediency in the broken condition of humanity as that is manifest in the broken body of Christ. In contemplating that broken body we are able to calibrate the terrible cost of crossing the chasm between the kingdom and the world. We grasp and envisage the human disfigurement of sin in the inhumane disfigurements of the crucifixion. This is what sin does and this is what sin means. Christ takes our burden upon him and falls and sinks under the weight of evil. Our losses are thrown into high relief in the figure of a burdened and tortured man. We recognise the primal violence that lies latent in ourselves and that we inflict on others in the violence wreaked on an innocent man. He has 'done nothing amiss' and yet he pays for the consequences. The vicious dynamic of sin understood as violence against each other rages like a contagion until, maybe, it discharges itself far from the point of origin on the head of the innocent. To reverse these losses the faithful absorb the broken body to share in the sacrificial act and to share in renewed communion with Christ and each other. They recapitulate the cost of crossing the chasm and by grace they are restored to full communion to become once more 'at one'.

Further Reflections

We begin with the reflection that both the blessedness of salvation and the recovery of wholeness depend on the blessedness of sin and on the disastrous act of separation from the unity of the divine. Without sin there can be neither human history as such nor a history of salvation. This reflection is built into a supreme moment in the liturgy of Easter Eve: *O blessed sin that merited so great salvation: O certe necessarium Adae peccatum, quod Christi morte deletum est,*

O felix culpa quae talem ac tantum meruit habere redemptorem.[4] Were 'the world' not at odds with 'the kingdom' and were Christianity not athwart 'the grain of the world' there could be no drama of salvation. What has never been broken in the arena of a broken world cannot be ransomed, healed, restored and forgiven. There could be no *joy in heaven over one sinner that repents* if there were no sin motivating repentance. The prodigal son could not be received back with grace and love apart from his departure to a far country in which *he would fain eat the husks that the swine did eat.* One cannot rejoice having no reason to rejoice.

There is an important corollary of the idea of 'blessed sin' which concerns time, change and scarcity, and all three have to be followed through in sequence. Time involves contingency in that everything is precarious and contingent. Everything grows, decays and dies. We often think that processes of maturation and decay, and the fragility of all we care about and desire, is matter for regret and lament: 'all flesh is as grass and all the glory of man as the flower of grass./ The grass withereth and the flower thereof falleth away'. But the ephemeral nature of what is desired is what makes it precious, lends it meaning and inspires our longing and what the German Romantic poets call *Sehnsucht.* That is why poetry is about love and loss.

But without maturation and death and without change and decay we would be condemned to eternal stasis. Without unattained desire there is no striving. That is why humans find it so difficult to imagine heaven since it is not clear how a state defined by absolute security and peace can be the summit of human desire. Nobody truly desires perpetual blossom time without harvest, even though we can expend a lifetime of regret for the evanescence of youth and, like the Chinese sage in a novel by Terry Pratchett, cherish a secret valley where change and decay are halted beyond the reach of maturation.

Here we need to turn to scarcity. In one way we lament scarcity because it means that millions of our fellow creatures lack the means to live abundantly. That is cause for lament just as the losses suffered by humanity are cause for lament. Nevertheless, scarcity is the precondition of value and satisfaction. If we have everything we value nothing. Value is forged against lack, our own and that of others. Scarcity is as much the source of dynamism as secure attainment would be the source of stasis. A famous short story, 'The Immortals', by Jorge Luis Borges, imagines the ennui that such stasis would entail. *'Wolle die Wandlung',*

---

[4]   There is a medieval version of this re-applied to the taking of the humanity of Mary into God, which may have an ironic edge. It is in the medieval carol 'Adam lay y-bowndyn' and runs 'Ne hadde the appil take ben .../Ne hadde never our Lady a ben hevene queen'.

'Desire all change', as Rainer Maria Rilke put it.[5] It is of the nature of religious desire to occupy the space between longing and attainment. Yet without the embodied experience of something approaching the yearned-for mutual recognition, based on fully knowing and being known, the human imagination would be unable to give any form to this ultimate attainment and mutuality. That is what lends power to the poetry of Francis Quarles based on the Song of Songs, where the poet imagines what it would be to enjoy a mutual possession: *My beloved is mine, and I am his; He feedeth among the lilies.*[6]

> He is my altar; I his Holy Place,
> I am his guest, and he my loving food;
> I am his by penitence; he is mine by grace;
> I'm his by purchase; he is mine by blood.

Thomas Traherne, in his *Centuries of Meditation*, imagines what it would be to enjoy perfect unity with the world where everything is 'at rest, pure and immortal'. But this moves us because it is an epiphanic vision of the moment not confirmed by quotidian living. It 'flashes upon our inward eye' but quickly retires to the margin of our ordinary apprehensions. Like the poetry of Francis Quarles it occupies the space between longing and attainment.

What I have been arguing about change, contingency and scarcity can best be caught in a musical metaphor, provided we do not take the metaphor as comprehensive. The 'world', to quote John Dryden, is full of 'jarring, jarring sounds', but music cannot move without discord. It begins with order, but it cannot proceed further without disorder.[7] Music runs through all the compass of possibilities and instabilities requiring interim resolution before it returns to the original generator of all these possibilities and instabilities. Browning, in

---

5   Rainer Maria Rilke '*Wolle die Wandlung*', Sonnet xii in *Sonnets to Orpheus by Rainer Maria Rilke*, trans. M.D. Herter Norton, New York: Norton, 2006.

6   Francis Quarles, 'My Beloved is Mine and I am His: He feedeth among the lilies', in D.H.J. Nicholson and A.H.E. Lee (eds) *The Oxford Book of English Mystical Verse*, Oxford: Clarendon, 1917, p. 21.

7   John Dryden. 'A Song for St. Cecilia's Day' (1687), in *The Golden Treasury*, ed. Francis T. Palgrave, London: Macmillan 1947, pp. 63–4. Dryden's text, ravishingly set by Handel nearly fifty years later, combines elements from the idea of the music of the spheres with ideas of the Last Judgement, but it provides a reminder that music not only reveals a fundamental harmony but 'excites us to arms'.

his poem 'Abt Vogler', marvellously traces the evolution of dissonances seeking resolution until they come to rest on 'the C major of this life'.[8]

Of course, we cannot take the musical metaphor as more than suggestive but if sin is disharmony then it is built into the movement of the drama. The drama of good and evil cannot even begin without it. Without time as the framework, musical contrast or progression would not be possible. Time and contingency are the generators of meaning and value and that includes the potential for loss. We value what is at risk in a broken world, and if there were no death we would not and could not value life at its true estimate. As for sin, it does not spring from desire directed towards a good end because desire is the source of all our motivating energies. Desire cannot be denied without breaking through with distorted power. The problem of desire is the problem of wrongly directed excess, especially in cultures that as a psychological and economic principle elevate the exponential expansion of desire over the achievement of satisfaction.

Here we should turn again to the desire for a restored unity with others after breakage of trust and denial. Atonement includes this desire for a restored unity. We should read the resurrection stories that conclude all the Gospels less as 'proofs' of a triumph over death and time as the recovery of table fellowship after it had been severed by breakages of trust. These stories summarise the experience of peace and restored fraternity. The revelation of the presence of Christ in the breaking of bread at Emmaus is linked with the revelation of his presence when he appears later that same evening to the assembled disciples with the offer of his peace: 'Peace be with you'. In both moments of revelation Christ restores lost fellowship and he grants peace to his friends as he does at the conclusion of every Eucharist. When he asks for meat it is not because he is hungry but because he desires to recover the interrupted communion of the Last Supper. At the Last Supper he promised that he would no more drink of the fruit of the vine until he drank it 'new' with his friends in the Father's kingdom. This is the First Supper of the restored kingdom. The disciples become again a fellowship of reconciliation as well as a community of the resurrection.

Exactly the same is true of the resurrection scenes in the closing passages of St John's Gospel. Jesus is initially an unrecognised presence before restoration is completed by actions that reverse and heal earlier breaches of trust. The disciples enjoy communion just as they enjoyed it when Jesus washed their feet in his final act of service. He asks them to behold his hands and his feet to understand that this is a God who has taken our infirmities into himself and knows what it is to

---

[8]   Robert Browning, 'Abt Vogler', in *Poems of Robert Browning*, Oxford: Oxford University Press, 1910, pp. 634–5.

suffer and to die. The face of the divine is a scarred face like all our human faces. We read divinity in the face of Christ. Christ has eaten of the bread of affliction and drunk of the dregs of human experience but he has renewed them through overflowing gifts of bread and wine in the fellowship of the kingdom. This is the Lord's best wine replacing the old.

If you seek him in the grave you look for him in the wrong place. '*Quem quaeritis in sepulchro?*' 'Whom do you seek in the sepulchre'/'Why seek ye the living among the dead? '*Non est hic.*' He is not here but anywhere where friends meet in his name and gather round his table.[9]

One thousand and six hundred years ago St John Chrysostom preached his paschal address for Easter Day. It was recited from memory by a monk in Dachau at Easter April 1945 without service books or vestments, except borrowed SS uniforms, immediately after the camp was relieved by the Americans.

> The Master is generous and accepts the last as the first.
> He gives rest to him that comes in the eleventh hour
> Even as he who laboured from the first.
> He accepts the deed and honours the intention.
> Rich and poor, dance together, you who fasted and you who did not fast,
> Rejoice together.
> The calf is fatted: let none go away hungry.
> Let none lament his poverty.
> For the universal kingdom is revealed.
> Let none bewail his transgressions,
> For the light of forgiveness has risen from the tomb.
> 'O death where is thy sting? O grave where is thy victory?
> Christ is risen and the demons are fallen.
> Christ is risen and the angels rejoice,
> Christ is risen and life reigns. Alleluia.'

---

[9]   This is, of course, the question (and answer) put in the Easter Liturgy over the last millennium.

Second Commentary

Speaking Christian, its Vocabulary and Grammar

The idea of 'speaking Christian' comes from the Australian poet Les Murray.[1] Murray is a Catholic and one of his collections is entitled *Learning Human*. Reading Les Murray I arrived by extension at the idea of speaking Christian. Of course, speaking Christian is a version of learning human, especially given that Christianity is quite literally a humanly embodied faith revealed in a human face. Its fundamental coinage is very familiar: words like water and blood, wine and bread, garden and city. Part of its vocabulary reflects the fundamentals of life in the Mediterranean: lamb, shepherd, vine, husbandman. There follow more abstract ideas like sin and holiness, grace and law, fall and redemption, judgement and forgiveness, bondage and liberation. Then there are concepts involving time and duration, beginnings and endings: for example, creation and recreation, advent (or proclamation) and fulfilment, the transition to a new life through death in the waters of baptism, the transition from the broken unity of the sacred meal to full communion and restored fellowship around the table. All these concepts rest on basic contrasts like the kingdom and 'the world'. Finally there is a governing sequence running from incarnation to atonement and from resurrection to ascension. It is the relation between these basic elements that is distinctive, and my argument assumes that wherever you begin a symbolic logic would lead to all the others. Speaking Christian has a grammar as well as a vocabulary.

The contrast between the kingdom and 'world' is a good place to begin because it embodies what I call the Christian angle of transcendence. You can gauge the angle of transcendence by grasping the difference between the life of the kingdom and the ways of 'the world'. An acute angle of transcendence is indicated by recognising the ways in which the kingdom radically revises the priorities and accepted practices of the world, for example with regard to the occasions and practice of violence. The contrast between the pursuit of the peace of the kingdom and the recourse to violence in the world provides a critical marker.

---

[1]   Les Murray, *Learning Human: New Selected Poems*, Manchester: Carcanet, 2001.

Christianity envisages stages whereby the world is overcome and the acute angle of transcendence cancelled. In the first stage the difference is overcome in principle. This occurs when the divine Word emerges in the world and the world does not recognise it; and again when the tribulation of the world is overcome by the Word and the kingdom of the lie crumbles at the advent of truth; and again when death is overcome by resurrection. The kingdom lies latent within the heart and as a secret seed burgeoning in time. The second stage hovers in the future as a potential for a time when 'God is all in all' and the heavenly city comes down from heaven above to dwell on earth among humankind. The prayer for the kingdom to come on earth as it is in heaven is answered and humankind is delivered from evil.

The contrast between the kingdom and the world generates eschatology, that is, a hope that one day faith may become sight, the real subsumed in the ideal and the world transformed into the kingdom. Given that the kingdom is in the future there are many versions of how that might come about. Maybe it would come unannounced and secretly, or maybe the seeds sown in the hearts of the faithful would slowly unfold, or maybe the kingdom would descend with an effulgent and unmistakeable glory on the Last Day and the Son of God inaugurate the Last Judgement. There is an oscillation discernible in the Gospels between a spiritual transformation and a cosmic transformation.

Much of the time the kingdom is inward and 'not of this world' but at other times the Son of Man and his angels will pour out the vials of judgement on the wicked. The anticipations of the Davidic kingdom that surface in the Gospels hint at a reversal of all those power structures that have so far favoured the Gentiles. This oscillation derives from varied intimations of eschatology in the later prophetic books of the Hebrew Scriptures. At the same time the angle of transcendence is much less acute in Judaism. For much of its history Judaism does not even entertain a hope of a transformed life after death. The initial contrast in the book of Genesis is not between physical and spiritual versions of eschatological hope but rather between chaos and creation, with a second creation hinted at in the face of the chaos represented by the flood. Eschatology only emerges and grows increasingly urgent with the failure of trust in God's physical deliverance from the hands of 'them that hate us', the inveterate enemies of Israel. The governing narrative is provided by the exodus from Egypt and that narrative appears borne out with the end of the Babylonian exile. From such extraordinary dramas of national and territorial liberation, at least as recounted in Scripture, it seems that God is after all faithful to his covenant with his chosen people. Isaiah, for example, in the sixtieth chapter of his prophecy anticipates the time when Israel shall hold her oppressors captive. Yet such an ecstatic expectation is time and again doomed to disappointment and in the psalms we can trace the oscillation between a hope of deliverance and despair that God is so tardy in redeeming his promises. A different line of thinking emerges in Isaiah appealing to the figure of the Suffering Servant of the Lord. The oscillation in the Gospels continues the oscillation visible in the Hebrew Scriptures between Israel as Suffering Servant and Israel as an imperial centre drawing from far and wide on the wealth of subject nations.

The idea of the Suffering Servant as it is appropriated in the Gospels entails a spiritualisation of the governing narrative of the exodus from oppression to liberty. An outward political deliverance becomes an inner spiritual transformation and it fosters the double entendre referred to earlier. The hope of a political restoration mutates into a regime based on service as symbolised by the master washing the feet of the disciples and by the annual sacrament repeated in every Holy Week of mastery realised in humility. This crucial mutation requires a spiritualisation of all the key concepts associated with the physical restoration of the glory of Israel. Jerusalem as the capital of the restored kingdom becomes the heavenly city, New Jerusalem, whose trees are 'for the healing of the nations'. The physical temple dissolves into the body of Christ where all the members of his body become pillars of a new spiritual building. Nevertheless the idea of a restored kingdom does not entirely disappear and the oscillation between territorial restoration and spiritual transformation continues throughout Christian history. That oscillation is traced in detail in the commentary focused on peace and violence.

Here I trace the symbolic logic of the inward and spiritual transformation as already illustrated in the symbols of the heavenly Jerusalem and the temple of Christ's body realised wherever two or three gather together in Christ's name. For that there is not better illustration than the controversy within the New Testament over the displacement of physical circumcision, understood as a rite literally incorporating the newborn in the people of Israel, by the rite of baptism as that effects a transition from an old life to new by a passage through water. In baptism, Christians die to their former selves as they are plunged, actually or symbolically, in the purifying waters and washed clean. In some rites they are re-clothed, as it were, in divine righteousness. Baptism entails a radical revision of all the occasions in the Hebrew Scriptures when the Israelites are saved by making a physical transition through water. The symbolic logic of the spiritual transformation or *metanoia* could hardly be more clearly illustrated.

This is where a Christian mode of interpretation (or hermeneutic) based on typological identifications overlaps anthropological structuralism. Supposing we begin with the Flood, the ark becomes the Church as the vehicle whereby the people of God are brought to safety. This interpretation is dramatically illustrated in Benjamin Britten's *Noyes Fludde*. The church is the ship (the word nave probably derives from the medieval Latin *navis* or ship) that carries the redeemed to safety. The same is true of the basket in the bulrushes whereby the threatened child is preserved from danger. The great and most dramatic transition occurs when the Children of Israel pass unharmed through the perils of the Red Sea and land safely on the other side. This transition is a 'type' or intimation of baptism in more than one way: the Christian passes safely through the waters of baptism to the further shore of redemption. Thus Handel's oratorio *Israel in Egypt* is both a celebration of the physical redemption of Israel and an Easter oratorio celebrating the passage of Christ through death to resurrection life. St John Damascene catches this precisely in his Easter hymn: 'Our Christ has brought us over with hymns of victory'. This passage through death to life eternal is replicated in the rite of baptism. A final example is provided by the baptism of Christ himself as prototype of the great transition or *metanoia* undergone by 'all found in him'. As Joshua, the great leader to the Promised Land, came to the moment when he crossed over Jordan 'to posses the Land', so Jesus, his namesake, came to the Jordan to be baptised and recognised as the Son of God who should redeem his people from their sins.

Just as the people of Israel wandered for the symbolic period of forty years in the wilderness, so Jesus, after his baptism, was 'driven by the Spirit' into the wilderness for forty days to be tempted by the Devil. These temptations represent the first confrontation of the kingdom with 'the world' because Jesus is tempted to use the ways of the world magically to inaugurate the kingdom. He is offered the whole world but refuses to gain it by obeisance to the 'Prince of this world' who offers what is not his to give.

Here we pick up another group of linkages associated with the displacement of circumcision by baptism. We have already seen that circumcision, as an operation ritually carried out on the genitals, signifies incorporation in the people of God elected by Covenant to be by birthright the object of his special care and protection. Baptism displaces the membership by birthright with a second birth in the Spirit. One might add here the symbolic meaning of the virgin birth 'by the spirit' as creating a new cell untainted by the Fall which can then replicate itself in all who undergo baptism into the new body of the Church. But whatever symbolic meaning one attributes to the Lucan story of the virgin birth, there is a clear displacement of physical birthright by the declared necessity of being born again 'by the Spirit'. In short, the physical continuity of the generations enjoying privileges within the covenant people of God becomes a unity in the Spirit of all who elect to undergo the waters of baptism.

I am here drawing attention to the symbolic logic underpinning spiritual as distinct from genetic brotherhood, and by extension, spiritual brotherhood as distinct from the brotherhood of arms. There is a fundamental rivalry between the spiritual brotherhood established by baptism and the divine gift of blood, the physical brotherhood established by blood relations, whether of close kin or the extended kinship of the tribe, and the brotherhood of arms based on a readiness to shed the blood of 'the Other'. Spiritual brotherhood inheres in all baptised Christians but it takes a specific form in the brotherhoods of the 'secular' priestly stratum and the brotherhoods and sisterhoods of professed monks and nuns. These spiritual brotherhoods are under vows of obedience to spiritual fathers, right up to the universal jurisdiction of the Pope as 'Holy Father'. These associations came to exercise enormous power, whether or not, like the Cistercians, they sought to abjure as far as possible the blandishments of 'the world'. The meek who pursued humility became collectively corporations exercising great power and accumulating great wealth. The meek really did 'inherit the earth'. These corporations express and represent a tension between the kingdom and the world. They cordon off and separate from the world those Max Weber called religious 'virtuosi'.

The Reformation sought to extend this tension from religious virtuosi to all the laity and in so doing relaxed the tension over sexuality represented by voluntary or enforced celibacy, however much that was 'honoured in the breach rather than the observance'. This specific tension of kingdom and world has to be dealt with in the commentary on sexuality just as the tension over violence has to be dealt with by a separate commentary. A further tension over the aesthetic, the Cistercians again providing a major example, would require a commentary I have not provided. I do not intend at this point to canvass the extent to which influences from eastern sources, including Eastern Christianity, contributed to a contempt for the world, and in particular the flesh, that gained momentum as Christianity was partly assimilated to the 'powers that be' in the fourth century ad. It is of some interest that Constantine delayed baptism until close to death given what was required of him in the interim as emperor. It was during the centuries following conversion to Christianity that the imperatives of the kingdom, for example with regard to possessions, were adjusted in this way, as analysed in the opening essay on Christianity 'against the grain of the world'.

We come now to the densest and richest of all symbolic concentrations of meaning in Christianity: the bread and wine of the Eucharist understood as a Christian adaptation and transformation of the Passover. We can begin with a simple typological transfer: the physical food provided by God for the people of God in the wilderness on their way to the Promised Land becomes the spiritual food of the body and blood of Christ for the baptised on their spiritual pilgrimage to the heavenly country. Here the contrast between the wilderness as a physical place and as a spiritual condition is quite clear, as is the contrast between promised territory and the pursuit of a spiritual destination which is to come. Jewish anticipation looks for 'next year in Jerusalem' whereas Christian scripture says plainly 'Here we have no abiding city but we seek one which is to come.' The city to come is the heavenly Jerusalem understood as the antitype of Babylon and the abode of peace and blessedness, as in Abelard's great hymn *O quanta qualia sunt illa Sabbata*. Christians are travelling from Babylon to Jerusalem (*et ad Jerusalem/a Babylonia*) and the restoration of Jerusalem's 'mighty Sabbaths' has lost its temporal as well as its spatial reference. The end of exile in the Hebrew Scriptures has become the end of our exile and our alienation from our true selves.

But as we contemplate the transformation of bread and wine into the body and blood of Christ the contrasts of physical and spiritual can seem less clear. Of course, bread and wine are part of the physical bounty of the earth, tilled and shaped by human hands, and they are transformed into the gifts of God offered to the people of God. Ordinary food and drink has become the body and blood latent in the sacramental elements, to adapt Thomas Aquinas in his hymn to the 'hidden God' *Adoro te devote latens Deitas/Quae sub his figuris vere latitas*. The contrast between the spiritual warfare of the kingdom and the Exodus from Egypt is very clear. On the one hand there is the physical deliverance of the Israelites from oppression in Egypt and on the other hand the spiritual victory over sin and death, understood as the powers of 'this world', wrought by Jesus Christ. The Christian understanding of this victory sees Christ as confronting worldly powers and paying the cost of redemption in his body. That cost is placarded in the brokenness and humiliation of the body of the Saviour. The cost is anticipated in the breaking of bread and the pouring out of the wine at the Last Supper and re-enacted in the breaking of bread and pouring out of wine in every Christian Eucharist since. The unity of table fellowship was broken by treachery and denial at the Last Supper and at the First Suppers after the Resurrection unity is restored by renewed table fellowship. There is first the declaration 'Peace be with you' and then the request to share once again in table fellowship 'Have you any meat?' We have a drama of brokenness as the powers of this world do their worst and of reunion and communion as Christians reassemble in renewed table fellowship.

Typologically the institution of the Eucharist shadows the institution of the Passover and the narrative of the Exodus quite closely. I have already indicated the typological shadowing of the crossing of the Red Sea understood as Christ's triumphant passage through the waters of death. But there are very clear typological parallels between the Passover narrative and the Passion narrative.

As the Bible tells the original story, and as the New Testament recapitulates it, the Israelites are saved by the blood of the Lamb on the lintel of the door and Christians are saved by the outpouring of the blood of the lamb on their behalf. In both cases death is thwarted by blood as the symbol of life. The difference lies in the identification of the sacrifice of the lamb with the self-giving of the Saviour for his people. The Lamb of God is the scapegoat that takes away and bears in his body the sins of 'the world'. To return to my original contrast, the powers of the kingdom and of its righteousness encounter and overcome in deadly battle the powers of evil in 'the world'. *Finita iam sunt proelia.* As the Scottish Franciscan poet William Dunbar put it:

> Done is the battle on the dragon black,
> Our champion Christ confounded has his force.[2]

This brings us to the transforming presence of the Son of God and the Son of Man within 'the world'. According to Christian faith the God who inhabits the harmonious life of highest heaven 'comes down' and becomes implicated with the way 'the world' is. The creator, who from his safe abode demands so much from humanity by way of righteousness, limits himself to share and face the tribulations of his creatures. He becomes, according to Paul in his Epistle to the Philippians 2:7, shorn and emptied of his glory to be present in and with humanity. In the language of John's Gospel chapter 1 he was in 'the world' incognito because the world 'did not know' him.

Here one does not have to rely solely on St John's understanding of the person of Christ. In rather abstract terms the acute angle of transcendence becomes immanent in the way things are. Here the break with Judaism is most striking because the God whose name cannot be spoken acquires a name and the God who cannot be imagined acquires a human face which is the 'express image' of the divine. In the Hebrew Scriptures 'no man may look on God and live' whereas in the New Testament the glory of God is revealed 'in the face of Jesus Christ'. The believer has 'both seen him and known him'. Our humanity has been taken into the Godhead and in Orthodox iconography the cosmos has been centred in the human face of the Pantocrator. Robert Browning caught this in is poem *Saul* where he speaks of encountering in the Godhead 'a Face like my face'.[3]

---

[2]   William Dunbar (?1465-1520), 'On the Resurrection of Christ', in Donald Davie (ed.) *The New Oxford Book of Christian Verse*, Oxford: Oxford university Press, 1981, pp. 21–2.

[3]   Robert Browning, 'Saul', in Browning, *Poems of Robert Browning*, p. 32.

This is where the kingdom of heaven is identified as 'in the world' and working within it for our redemption. The kingdom comes in order to recover our losses. What humanity lost in the first Adam is regained in the second Adam. This included the defeat of death, as the grim reality that dominates 'the world', through the saving death and resurrection of Christ: 'For as in Adam all die, even so in Christ shall all be made alive', and that enlivening includes renewed spiritual life through baptism. Some of the seventeenth-century English metaphysical poets expressed this perfectly. William Fuller captured Christian doctrine by echoing the Psalmist's question 'What is man that thou art mindful of him?'

> Lord, what is man, lost man, that thou shouldst be so mindful of him
> That the Son of God forsook his glory, his abode
> To become a poor tormented man!
> The deity was shrunk into a span,
> And that for me, O wondrous love, for me! ...
> That man should be assumed into the deity
> That for a worm a God should die?[4]

Here we have the pattern that governs the relation of heaven above to 'the world' beneath to bring them together beyond dissolution: the pattern of descent and ascent whereby Heaven in the person of Christ descends to Humanity, or condescends, to use an older word, and takes humanity into God. The creed is structured around this pattern of descent and ascent as well as the pattern of the Trinity identifying the work of Christ with the divine action in 'the world'. In New Testament terms 'He that descended is he that ascended'. The spatial imagery sounds mythic but the message it conveys concerns the identification of the transcendent in our flesh and blood, Emmanuel, 'God with us'. Again a poet, Isaac Watts, grasps this in a phrase clearly echoing the Athanasian creed: 'Our God contracted to a span/Incomprehensibly made man.' That taking of humanity into God is realised in the idea that Christ re-presents us before God and takes with him into God the shocking marks of his deadly encounter with evil. Humanity exalted and transfigured is disfigured by that encounter. The poet refers to 'that dear disfigured face'. Our 'high priest', to adapt the Epistle to the Hebrews, stands for us a wounded man in the holy place. Our losses have been absorbed in the body of Christ. Here we come back to the brokenness of the

---

4   William Fuller, 'A Divine Hymn', set to music in 1688 by Henry Purcell (Z 192) as part of Purcell's *Harmonia Sacra II*.

body of Christ in the Eucharist that restores all the participants to an unbroken communion as they receive the 'medicine of immortality'. Each Christian sign folds back into all the others in a circle of mutual reinforcement.

'Learning Christian' includes absorbing this pattern of descent and ascent. 'He that descended is also he that ascended.' But it also includes a rather different vocabulary of Nature and Grace, as well as Law and Grace. Using this vocabulary Christians speak of Christ 'taking our nature upon him'. Our nature is mired in sin understood as separation from communion with God and alien to ourselves. But what is sin? Many Christians baulk at the idea that they are sinful or else they identify sinfulness with peccadilloes. Nevertheless the project of 'learning Christian' does require us to give some account of what is meant by our 'sinful nature'. It also requires us to give some account of what we mean by judgement. Judgement, like sin, encounters considerable resistance from people used to a therapeutic approach where judgement is equated with being self-righteously judgemental and fulsome admission of sinfulness equated with chronic lack of a sense of self-worth. The old formula *mea culpa, mea maxima culpa* or the words of confession in the *Book of Common Prayer* have no psychological purchase and awake no flicker of inner recognition.

There are various translations of the tension between the kingdom and the world or between sin and salvation. They are reaching the mark and failing to reach it, or the fragmented and the whole, the broken and the restored, the flawed and the renewed, the inauthentic and the authentic, the bound and the liberated, and the love of self as contrasted with love of neighbour. Becoming authentic leans towards relief from the individual and existential kinds of sinfulness, whereas becoming liberated leans towards release from the social and structural kinds of sinfulness. The experience of relief and of liberation may be dramatic, as in some accounts of conversion, but it can also be incremental and continuous, otherwise renewed confession would make no sense. Luther had a strong sense of being simultaneously enslaved by sin and liberated by grace: *Simul iustus et peccator*, at once most surely a sinner and most surely justified.

'Worldliness', as in John Bunyan's figure of Mr Worldly Wiseman, is entrapped and seduced by the vanities that distract him in Vanity Fair. It has to do with false priorities, and here the key text in the New Testament is 'Seek ye first the kingdom of God and his righteousness and all these other things will be added unto you.' There are also softer versions of the tension in the contrast a moral philosopher, (say) Bishop Joseph Butler, might make between self-love and benevolence or the contrast psychologists might make between instinctual self-concern and altruism. According to these softer versions the language of evil is moderated to notions like 'out of order' or unacceptable. For Christianity there remains a high tension between self-involvement, enslavement or rebellion and salvation, and Shakespeare firmly expressed the conflict of rival powers within the Christian soul in his sonnet 146:

> Poor soul, the centre of my sinful earth,
> The rebel powers that thee array.

The Christian account of sin and judgement is paradoxical. Sin is endemic and universal but grace is all-sufficient. One may not judge others in case one traps oneself in the same judgement, 'judge not that ye be not judged', but nevertheless moral discrimination between good and evil requires judgement, otherwise the moral world collapses. One is unable to name the unspeakable inhumanity of human beings towards their fellows. Even in the therapeutic context where one seeks healing and recognition of fault by initially suspending judgement, one has to identify the difference between the proper use and improper or 'inappropriate' abuse of others. In the Christianity of the period suspended between the pagan and the Christian, pastors and bishops warned of irruptions from the 'other world' that acted as an interim judgement prior to the Last Judgement.

Inappropriate abuse is a contemporary translation of sin. Sin is both an ineradicable aspect of our humanity and an ineradicable idea within the Christian vocabulary. 'Learning Christian' begins here. If we try to evade it by expunging the word it resurfaces in our pseudo-scientific linguistic usage in terms like pathological and dysfunctional, let alone omnibus un-selfconscious terms like victim, disgrace and 'corruption'. Disgrace is parasitic on the idea of grace, just as the idea of the victim requires the idea of the perpetrator.

Sin and salvation are cognate with law and grace. The concept of sin depends on the existence of law otherwise you have nothing to sin against, and salvation means being covered by grace and showing the fruits of grace. So there is a natural transition from any account of sin and salvation and an account of law and grace. In turning now to law and grace I need to set them within my contrast between the kingdom and the world and against the backdrop of Christianity as coding an acute angle of tension with the world. Of course, I am aware that from the fourth century to the present this has been hotly contested territory and I have to tread warily.

Perhaps I should begin with law understood as the social necessity of moral regulation as opposed to the kind of anarchic chaos where everyone 'does right in his own eyes'. This kind of moral regulation requires no religious sanction or source. One has only to canvass the alternative to be aware of the necessity of law. Once authority becomes weak and capricious no one is safe and everyone is forced to concentrate on defence at the expense of the arts of peace. The 'war of all against all' as formulated by Thomas Hobbes is only one dramatic expression of that alternative and it includes by extension the social necessity of a settled acceptance of authority. Shakespeare makes precisely the same point about authority in some famous lines in *Troilus and Cressida*:

> Take but degree away, untune that string,
> And, hark, what discord follows, each thing meets
> In mere oppugnancy.

As argued earlier, Shakespeare is clear that right and wrong, justice and injustice lose their names and are eaten up by appetite and power, and by the appetite for power. In his 'problem play' *Measure for Measure* Shakespeare plays with the oscillation between moral chaos and settled authority. The conclusion of the play is recognised as morally ambiguous when the Duke distributes mercy randomly to several kinds of delinquent without prior exercise of justice. Moral discomfort arises from the arbitrary nature of the Duke's decisions and one is left wondering whether this might usher in another descent into the 'anything-goes' chaos from which the premise of the play's narrative arose. Authority does not have to be authoritarian, as is often supposed, but it does require settled competences, responsibilities and procedures and these have to be internalised in habits handed on from generation to generation through tradition. Authority is always open to abuse but without authority no civilised existence is possible. People need to have secure expectations, and a conservative gloss on this existential requirement claims that 'the onus of proof lies on the proposers of change'.

These are arguments drawn from secular reason and ordinary worldly wisdom. They acknowledge what must happen if human beings are reduced to living in a state of nature. Contemporary people sometimes play with the notion of anarchy and treat all settled arrangements as up for endless discussion as inherently oppressive, but that is because the safety guaranteed by advanced standards of living permits intellectual dalliance. As T.S. Eliot pointed out in a chorus in *The Rock*: 'It is hard for those who live near a Bank/To doubt the security of their money.'[5]

For any faith that codes an acute angle of tension between the world as it might be and 'the kingdom', there has to be a compromise with things as they are. I hesitate to attribute my argument here to Augustine but I imagine it to

---

[5]   T.S. Eliot, from *The Rock*, in *T.S. Eliot: Collected Poems 1909–1962*, London: Faber & Faber, 1963, p. 174.

be broadly Augustinian in its recognition of a need for institutions that act as bulwarks against anarchy. The new law, as set out in the Sermon on the Mount and elsewhere in the Gospels, cannot be instituted here and now and it is set forth in the context of expectation of a new order instituted by God. Specifically the Gospel points to a new mode of living through hyperbole and pithy sayings that challenge ordinary ways of thinking. They are not remotely a comprehensive political blueprint such as is promulgated in Islam.

The Gospel challenges the institutions of reciprocal violence embodied in the *lex talionis*, it challenges the institutions of insurance and forethought for the future in order to live in the present, and it challenges the accumulation of wealth at the expense of the poor. It also demands that people forgive their enemies not just seven times but seventy times seven. In other words forgiveness, like humility and compassion, is endless. Every now and then it grimly comments on the way of a world where you need to make friends with 'the mammon of unrighteousness' and where 'To him that hath shall be given and to him that hath not even what he hath shall be taken away'. Notoriously the infant church even experimented with the community of goods. At the same time the early church had to devise ways of securing continuity in its procedures and to regulate disputes among Christians. And it had to formulate its relation to the old law of statutes and ordinance as set out in the Hebrew Scriptures. Those statutes, including circumcision, had been the focus of the identity of Israel and the Church claimed a universal identity based on the practices of love among the brethren as found in redistribution secured by the diaconate and in the shared meal of table fellowship and the Eucharist.

The Church also had to formulate an attitude to the 'powers that be' as in some sense necessary for society, but not in such a way as to compromise an ultimate appeal to God and to conscience. The saying in the Book of Acts claiming that 'we must obey God rather than men', and the Gospel judgement that distinguished between the things that belonged to God and those of Caesar, had enormous implications. The universal Church was set on a collision course with the universal empire because Christians cherished martyrs who among many other things could not take the oath of allegiance, the 'sacramentum', to the emperor. The dichotomy in Christian cultures between the two cities and also between the two swords was written in. Particularly in the Western Church there developed a distinction between spiritual and temporal.

Here we need to return from the distinction between temporal and spiritual to the tension between law and grace, particularly as formulated by St Paul. For Paul we press towards the mark but we miss the mark through sin and what he calls 'the law in our members'. Obviously this law of our sinful nature is very different from the 'law that is in ordinances'. In agreement with some classical thinkers Paul in Romans 7:19 regrets that 'the good I would I do not but the evil I would not, that I do'. We are at war with our own best desires and we are the site of struggle between good impulses upward and some remarkably powerful downward impulses. In some places Paul identifies this downward pull of our sinful nature with the body, as in his tortured cry 'Who shall deliver me from the body of this death?' The answer he gives is that Christ has overcome the law of sin and death and offers release through grace to all who are 'in him'. Paul may be defeated but through the grace of God and his love he becomes 'more than conqueror'. The 'law' condemns him in two ways, first by subjecting him to the sway of impulses and second by subjecting him to the demands and requirements of 'the law' which he is unable to fulfil.

Paul has much more to say. We may seek to fulfil the demands of the law but miss its spirit. Thus we may engage in extraordinary feats of moral heroism and self-control and miss the one thing necessary, which is love and charity. Our efforts must be informed by charity or we are no more than 'sounding brass and tinkling cymbals'. Beyond that, we cannot come before God making claims based on having fulfilled the law's demands. We cannot tot up our good works to present them as justifying us before the holiness of God. To seek justification on our own account, through boasting of our own achievements implies that we have achieved salvation through our own good works. Salvation is not secured by moral effort and striving to be righteous. Good works ought to flow from salvation but we cannot cite them as the basis of our justification.

We are, says Paul, in a lapidary formulation 'justified by faith, and that not of ourselves, it is the gift of God'. And the gift of God is realised in the cross, which is the all-sufficient sign and seal of God's infinite grace and love towards us. We are saved by responding to the gift in faith and trust. 'All our righteousness is as filthy rags' if we seek self-justification when what matters is the restoration of a broken relationship through our response to an 'inestimable gift'. Moreover, we are not saved by outward conformity but by an inward conversion of the spirit. This marks a profound shift from outer to inner already present in Judaism, whereby the law is reduced in its fundamentals to love of God and neighbour and turns on inward sincerity rather than outward conformity. Of course, there is a sense in which this increases pressure on individuals because you can know with some confidence that you have behaved according to the rules, whereas the extent of one's sincerity is subject to no obvious external standard.

So far we have been contrasting the law given in statutes as a defence against reversion to mere anarchy 'loosed upon the world', and the kingdom of grace where forgiveness is offered as a divine gift which we try to emulate in our lives by forgiving as we have been forgiven. We try to reverse the vicious spiral of negative reciprocity by a virtuous cycle of forgiveness. If that is to be fully realised in people's lives it needs to be founded on recognition of the wrong-doing that undermined a relationship and damaged the potential for communion with each other. Recognition implies penitence and a desire to make good and restore what has been mutilated and broken. It is precisely here that the acute angle of transcendence in Christianity seeking to recover and restore the lost runs into the limits on forgiveness set by our social nature.

Once third parties are involved, forgiveness cannot be endless. For example, you cannot forgive someone who has embezzled your funds. If that person is not named as having committed a criminal act, you effectively give him or her an anonymity to embezzle the funds of someone else. A priest who misuses his office to abuse children has to be disciplined not only on account of the failure to live up to the responsibilities of his office but to protect others from such behaviour. The priest may be given opportunity to redeem himself in due course but there has first to be acknowledgement and penitence, otherwise the flag of truth is not planted in the soul or raised in society at large. Pope John Paul II was able to visit his would-be Bulgarian murderer in prison and offer him personal forgiveness on a one-to-one basis, but he would not be able to behave in the same way to a Vatican official who misused the funds of the Bank of the Holy Spirit. Social justice and the integrity of institutions in the public realm have to trump personal forgiveness.

In the same way political life is and has to be unforgiving if public standards are to be upheld. A member of a legislature who makes false claims to emoluments has to pay the cost in terms of the ruin of his or her career, otherwise the integrity of politics itself is compromised. The political leader of a developing country is in no position to forgive a global corporation that casually pollutes the environment and causes the death of thousands of citizens. On the contrary, it is his moral duty, in the words of the New Testament, to ensure that the corporation 'pays to the uttermost farthing'. In such cases there is what one has to call strict moral entailment. The impossibility of extending forgiveness in politics includes failure to deliver, in the sense of achieving success. It is, of course, perfectly possible to commiserate privately with a politician who has led his or her party to successive defeats, but members of that party have to exact the price of failure for the sake of the party's future. That principle holds across the whole range of political action.

To put the matter in the framework of my argument here about the tension between the 'kingdom' and the 'world', politics is a realm in which the ways of the world negate the imperatives of the kingdom. There is, of course, a contemporary movement to ask for, or to offer, forgiveness between countries that have inflicted gross injuries on each other in peacetime as in war, or between violent factions within a society, and processes of this kind have a clear Christian motivation. The procedures of Peace and Reconciliation Commissions seek to implement at least some of the imperatives of the 'kingdom' but the warfare has to be securely over before such moves can be successfully initiated and before any of the price of murderous violence or complicity in the laws of an unjust state can be remitted in the name of reconciliation. One might add, that it is too often the case that those who offer retrospective political forgiveness have not suffered injustice themselves and that those they collectively forgive are not those who committed the injustice in the first place. The paradox is that peace and justice are often at war. Such a paradox serves to summarise the tension between the 'kingdom' and the 'world' that is the central theme of my argument.

Third Commentary

On Universal Love over against the Particular Family and Ethnic Group; and on Sex and Violence

If Christianity were 'with the grain' of social nature there would be no difficulty about eliciting its approach to the manifest problems of regulating sexuality. It would recognise sexuality as an absolutely central aspect of social life, both in its capacity to bind together in solidarity and violently to divide, and it would set out a responsible and realistic ethic for its optimum control and regulation. When anthropologists study a tribe or a cult they treat sexuality, social reproduction, kinship obligations and lineages as topics of central importance. After all, sex – and gender, its cultural analogue – is constitutive of personal identity and infiltrates every aspect of the individual's response to life. It also determines the limits of one's life trajectory, most dramatically in the case of the exchange of women which has been a central feature of many societies. The fact that the Apostles operated in a society where only men could be candidates for an intimate circle of discipleship is actually used in some circles to defend an exclusively male priesthood. The participation of women is clearly present in the Gospels but has not historically been given the prominence it deserves on account of exactly the same estimate of what are the appropriate roles of men and women.

The surprising thing is that if we were to take the Gospels, in particular the narrative of the Passion, as normative, there would be virtually no indications whatever of how a nascent religion proposed to negotiate and regulate the problems of sexuality. Forgiving seventy times seven may be recommended to a vengeful world but it hardly offers a viable jurisprudence in the matter of sexual regulation. It seems that the acute angle of transcendence characterising Christianity foreshortens time to the point where the imperatives of social reproduction so central to Judaism barely matter.

By contrast politics and power are a central matter of concern in the Gospels. After all, if Josephus is to be believed, the Gospels tell a story that takes place in a highly politicised environment and political sensitivities may well help account for the crucifixion. At the same time, the politics of the Gospels are opposed to political action. The same angle of transcendence that makes sexual regulation irrelevant requires an explicit repudiation of political action. There is nothing in the Gospels beyond generalised commitments to charity, justice and service that would help the disciple negotiate a naughty world or arrive at negotiated settlements. The kingdom is 'within you' and is 'not of this world'.

Here we need to recapitulate the argument governing the initial essay and all the commentaries. According to Karl Jaspers the Axial Age in the millennium before Christ was defined by a reserve about 'the world' which took various forms in different civilisations both East and West. According to Max Weber this reserve manifested different angles of transcendence expressed in every sphere of social life, the political, the economic, the aesthetic and the sexual. Each manifestation of reserve is closely linked with all the others, something we easily recognise in the link between sex and political violence. These commentaries suppose that reserve towards violence provides a critical marker, given that the oppressions of wealth and power are all based on the use of violence, either overt or covert.

The growth of a reserve towards 'the world' and towards our social nature is manifest in the growing difference between Judaism and what eventually emerges from Judaism as Christianity. That difference is summed up in an increasingly acute angle of eschatological tension represented by emergent Christianity, in particular the spiritualisation of the governing images of Judaism. By governing images I mean the exodus and the exile, the journey through the wilderness and the advent of the kingdom, and the symbolic role of the city and of the temple. These are all given spiritual meanings in Christianity, though there are notable reversions within Christianity to the original material meanings. In other words the double entendre within Christianity, on account of casting governing images loose from their material moorings, becomes obscured or lost. The kingdom reverts to an ordinary kingdom on earth and Jerusalem becomes once more a sacred city and site of pilgrimage.

This reversion to material meanings is most easily traced and understood in the economic sphere as described by Peter Brown in *Through the Eye of a Needle* and *The Ransom of the Soul*.[1] Peter Brown brings out the tension with 'the world' and our social nature generated by Christian teachings about wealth. In the words of Robert Browning, Christian teaching in this area, as elsewhere, is 'for earth too hard'.[2] This means that Christians will seek to find ways round

---

[1]   Brown, *Through the Eye of a Needle*; Brown, *Ransom of the Soul*.

[2]   Browning, 'Abt Vogler', in *Poems of Robert Browning*, pp. 634–6: 'The high that proved too high, the heroic for earth too hard.'

it, notably by emptying it of its spiritual reference and reverting to a material interpretation. Brown describes how fourth-century Christians interpreted 'treasure in heaven' as so much guaranteed real estate that would insure their future in the afterlife. That we find easy to understand. However, we find it less easy to grasp a similar tension in the sphere of sexuality, in spite of the fact that all the different spheres intimately intersect. In the contemporary climate we do not follow through the implications of Christian economic teaching any more than we follow through its teaching about violence, but we do accord these teachings respect as an ideal. They are officially 'on the books' of our civilisation and are accepted maybe as a desirable vision of a better world. The contemporary position with regard to sexuality is rather different. For example, we find a leading and respected historian, Diarmaid MacCulloch, with some sympathy for Christianity, at least as preached by Jesus, making a contrast in the course of a three-part TV series between the innocent pleasure of sex in the classical world with the encroachments of control and the repressive regimes introduced from the East into original Christianity.[3] Yet this is a shocking simplification and obviously not the case. The stories of Medea, Phaedra, Lucretia, Helen of Troy and Dido hardly testify to innocent sexuality. If I may take other examples from renaissance and baroque opera, sexuality in Monteverdi's *L'Incoronazione di Poppea* and in Handel's *Aggripina* and *Guilio Cesare* was as intimately bound up with power and violence as it was in Christendom in the times of Eleanor of Aquitaine. Innocent sexuality is an extraordinary modern myth, especially given all the evidence the modern world has of it.

The acute angle of eschatological tension in Christianity creates a reserve about the family and marriage that embarrasses forms of Christianity that have learnt to live in the world as it is. The Gospel clearly says there is no marriage in heaven but the Church has to operate on earth. Paul concedes that it 'is better to marry than to burn' and be consumed with lust, but the concession is distinctly reluctant. The reason behind this is very understandable. Where the angle of eschatological tension is acute, time is foreshortened to the point where the continuity of physical generation and the continuity of the generations over time hardly matters. It does not matter who begat whom, though the principle of continuity always lies latent in Christianity. The Christian Gospel actually begins with a genealogy to demonstrate its roots in Judaism, except that the genealogy passes through Joseph in order, presumably, to protect the claim that Jesus is 'of the house and lineage of David'.

---

3   *Sex and the Church*, BBC Two, May 2015.

It is in this matter of genealogy that Christianity diverges so sharply from its Judaic origins. Judaism emphasises the promises made to the forefathers, Abraham, Isaac and Jacob, 'and to their seed for ever'. The seed of the forefathers shall become as numerous as the sands of the seashore. Judaism celebrates fertility and is horrified by barrenness. The Christian *Magnificat* sung by Mary at the happy prospect of a child looks back to these Judaic roots, in particular the joy in the gift of children in the earlier celebrations of the unlikely childbirth of Sarah and Hannah. Of course, Christianity emphasises spiritual rebirth rather than physical continuity: 'You must be born again.' The virgin birth of Christ can be read as the formation of a new cell free of the transmitted taint of sin and death. But Christ is also identified as the summation of the Hebrew prophets.

We must begin with sex and violence as embedded in 'the world' and in our social nature. Up to the advent of the Axial Age religion reflected the powers of sex and violence and carried forward the will-to-power and domination. The temple at Karnak in Egypt is an architectural realisation of sheer brute power achieved by violence, and many of the deities of India express sexual power and sexual motifs. But with the Axial Age a new religious language emerged challenging the unrestrained expression of sex and violence and wealth and power. We have now to follow the logic of that challenge as it relates to the family and the ethnic group and to the impulse towards universal brotherhood.

The impulse to universal brotherhood and sisterhood, as it emerges in Christianity, requires the withdrawal of affect and affection from the family and its reattachment to the universal family of the Church. This redirection of affect is always very hard to maintain, though we can probably trace its influence when it comes to the relative unimportance of family liturgies in Christianity compared with Judaism. In Judaism the family as part of the ethnic group provides the religious nucleus. The exception to this is found in an early Protestantism that in some ways reverts to a more Judaic view of marriage and turns the home into a church and the head of the family into a priest.

The same problem arises in the Christian attitude to the ethnic group given that ethnic belonging, along with family belonging, provides the core of Jewish identity. Judaism is the faith of a people, and that faith is based on their specific covenant relation with God. Inevitably this relation breeds a sense of being a chosen people among the nations, which is liable to cause tension with other ethnicities not so uniquely favoured. Unique favour spells exceptional trouble.

The covenant relation protects Jewish identity and makes it uncomfortably obvious to others. It also provides a model to which Christianity sometimes reverts. The universal nation of the Church reverts to the ethnic model, so that the New Israel in some Bible-based cultures looks suspiciously like another version of the Old Israel, and the Christian family is conceived once again on the patriarchal model. Nations like America and Britain conceive of themselves as new Israels and provide favourable environments for Christian Zionism. They share with the old Israel the providential benefits accruing to a divinely favoured Zion.

Here we come to those verses in the Gospels that specifically repudiate the claims of the family of descent. Jesus asks 'Who is my brother and who is my sister?' 'The neighbour' in Christianity is anyone in need, irrespective of origin. Most disturbingly, Jesus in the Gospels says that anyone who puts family loyalty above loyalty to him is not worthy of him. This repudiation of the primacy of family ties is one of the sayings of Jesus which mark a radical shift of perspective transferring loyalty to the universal brotherhood. However uncomfortable this may be from the viewpoint of 'family values' we have no reason to doubt its authenticity and it is backed up by similar sayings elsewhere. Of course, Jesus remains throughout a devout Jew respecting the law whose special mission is to his own people. But his sayings point beyond the claims of the Jews as an ethnic group. If taken literally they also appear to subvert the Law on which all Jewish life ought to be based.

So we need a hermeneutic to make sense of these sayings, beginning with the evident use of hyperbole. This takes different forms. For example it is not literally the case that a man who 'offends against these little ones' should suffer a worse fate than having a millstone hung around his neck and 'cast into the depths of the sea'. Again, in his dialogue with 'the rich young ruler' Jesus makes a demand that he should sell all he has and 'give to the poor'.[4] This is not a demand he makes of everybody. The rich young ruler is proud of his adherence to the law 'from his youth up' and Jesus is saying that he has kept the letter of the law but not its inner spirit. He lives according to the law but is attached to his 'great possessions' and these overwhelm and choke his aspiration to 'eternal life'. It does not follow that everyone has to give all that they have to the poor.

There are other uses of hyperbole. With respect to the text about 'hating father and mother', if that were taken literally it would contravene the fifth commandment about honouring your father and mother. Jesus elsewhere commends the commandments so he is presumably indicating a priority. The family is not the *only* locus of loyalty compared with the priorities of the Gospel and the kingdom. Exactly the same point arises with respect to the man who asked leave to bury his father before becoming a disciple. This is an entirely

---

4   David Martin, 'Difficult Texts: Matthew 10.37', *Theology*, 118(2) (March/April 2015): 115–17.

proper request based on respect for parents but it elicits from Jesus one of his most striking sayings about the urgency of the kingdom and its priorities. 'Let the dead bury their dead.' Jesus says that the man who puts his hand to the plough and then looks back is not fit for the kingdom. Once again Jesus speaks of an unequivocal commitment to the reign of God, and the demand takes the form of hyperbole.

Of course, people are curiously literal minded, as we saw in the case of these early Christians who interpreted 'treasure in heaven' as so much real estate laid up for the future. Hyperbole is a dangerous literary form. But if Jesus had restricted his sayings to literal statements like 'it might be better if you did not rush to judgement when you yourself are vulnerable' or 'remember to treat little ones with appropriate respect' we should never have sat up and taken notice. Nevertheless if you compare one saying with another it becomes clear how Jesus understands the demands of the coming kingdom compared to other commitments. If people seek first the kingdom of God 'all these other things will be added unto them'. Now that is a statement of principle with characteristically radical implications and it is to those implications that we need to attend. Above all they concern power, not sexuality: the temptations of Jesus in the wilderness are solely concerned with power. By contrast, the temptations of the desert fathers in their search for the pure life of the spirit divested of bodily distractions are solely about sex. This codes the continuing tension within Christianity about conceptions of the kingdom, given that Jesus never concretely describes the kingdom but only indicates what it is 'like'. His intimate relationships with both women and men are construed in terms of loving affection with all sorts, with the woman at the well or with Nicodemus by night. He is not an ascetic but 'comes eating and drinking' and he anticipates eating and drinking together with his friends in the coming kingdom. The doctrine of the Incarnation deals precisely with the embodiment of God and the Gospels talk of living water and living bread. It is creaturely and its sense of the sublime is realised in creatureliness.

There is an important sense in which Christianity both spiritualises governing images and is profoundly materialistic in its emphasis on embodiment in the things of earth. It could not be more different from Islam, which forbids any image of the divine, but has a prophet who marries and fights. In other words Islam is not a religion with an Axial reserve about sex and violence. It reverts to something like Judaism but reconfigured as a universal faith. Jesus neither fights nor marries. That is crucial.

Again, unlike Islam, Christianity is not a social regime or even a doctrinal scheme but offers perspectives on the urgency of choice in the anticipated event of the coming of the kingdom. As far as explicit social regulation goes it is an open space of alarming freedoms governed only by the imperatives of discipleship and service. It is the narrative of the arrival of the kingdom culminating in the story of the Passion and Resurrection where the kingdom triumphs over the world. Given the acute angle of eschatological tension and the imminence of the rule of God, there was no need for an account of social regulation with respect to the quotidian problems of negotiating the world as it currently is, including the vital area of sexuality. And sexuality is vital because it is a focus of social reproduction and of social division. It is a source of every kind of power built into social nature, yet the Gospels have virtually nothing to say about it beyond the prohibition on divorce on account of men's 'hardness of heart'.

The pervasive influence of eschatological hope simply expresses itself in the option of voluntary celibacy, but it is obvious that no continuing society can be built on that option. The Gospels envisage some people opting for celibacy for the sake of the kingdom, and this later provides a basis of monasticism and for clerical celibacy. We are left with the uncertain implications of St John in chapter 8 where Jesus protects the woman 'taken in adultery' from stoning and simply tells her to 'sin no more'. Like the command about forgiveness, that is not any kind of foundation for a realistic sexual ethic.

This brings us to St Paul and the various models of appropriate sexual behaviour in the Bible, then undergoing the slow process of formalisation into a canon. Under the pressure of the oversight of widely flung Christian communities Paul turns to the available ready-mades in Judaism and in Roman law while at the same time suspecting they have a limited and interim utility given the approach of the Last Judgement. He stresses some combination of female submission and reciprocity within marriage, though he also recommends the voluntary celibacy he himself practises. Otherwise he echoes the patriarchal assumptions of his Jewish and Roman context. In the early Christian Church marriage was regarded as a personal and family affair and it was only in the eleventh century that the Church successfully claimed jurisdiction over marriage and even later that the Church defined marriage as an indissoluble sacrament. One of the motives of the early Church, as Peter Brown has argued, was to control the transmission of property from generation to generation, including donations to the church to secure immortality.[5]

---

5   I have not in this Commentary attempted to summarise the complex historical arguments made by Peter Brown about the spiritual value placed on sexual renunciation in the early centuries of Christianity as an anticipation of the resurrected body as part of the realisation of the eschatological kingdom. Brown cites John Chrysostom for whom virginity was evidence that 'the things of the resurrection stand at the door'. Peter Brown, *The Body and Society: Men, Women and Sexual Renunciation in Early Christianity*, London:

Yet sex remained a dubious activity even though marriage was a sacrament. It even remained problematic within marriage if pursued with too much lustful enthusiasm. Celibacy had become a required condition for the clergy in the Western Church, though not in the Eastern Church. In the great monastic orders, now centres of wealth and power, the great commandment concerned only the love of God so that affect was redirected to the figure of the Virgin Mary, and the Song of Songs in particular treated as an allegory of the love between Christ and the Church. Mary absorbed the affections of the universal spiritual brotherhoods. As for the generality of people in Christendom, clerical rules were often disregarded and it is obvious from medieval literature that a courtly love flourished based on adultery, and that clerics often disported themselves like lay persons.

A great change came with the Reformation and with the restoration of the Bible as an authority greater than clerical tradition. In one way the Bible was a great leveller because it was open and 'perspicuous' to a priesthood of all believers, even if what believers found in it was contentious and not always conducive to more equal marital relationships. The possibility of divorce, in England initiated by the monarch's need for an heir, served the interests of men but the *Book of Common Prayer* now affirmed that marriage was a contract for the mutual comfort and society of the man and the woman. The moral imperative of mutual comfort, derived from Bullinger, was only third among 'the purposes for which marriage was ordained' but it was accepted as a central characteristic of the marriage bond. Great clerics like Luther and Cranmer became married and the restoration of marriage to the clergy meant that the celibacy was downgraded. The home itself became a church in miniature and a centre of *koinonia*.

With the rise of Pietism and Evangelicalism women took an increasing role in matters of faith, even in some cases, like the Methodist Sarah Crosby, being allowed to preach. Evangelicalism is a highly personal religion focused on experience, and it included the enthusiastic singing of congregational hymns, often with erotic imagery, and the loving dialogue of the soul with God in Jesus Christ, the 'lover' of the soul. As in the past, marriage and lineage remained a major concern of social elites who used marriage strategies to consolidate family property and access to power of various kinds. For the lower classes informal 'marriage' or customary co-habitation was an option.

Faber, 1988, p. 442. In the same book Brown shows that the development of monasticism and the increased dominance of members of the social elite in monastic institutions and leadership of the Church had the effect of breaking the connection between elite status and the perpetuation of private family power and wealth.

The remaining story from the eighteenth century on concerns the declining ability of the churches, particularly the monopolistic established churches, to control marriage and the expression of sexuality. That happened dramatically in France with the Revolution and the institution of civil marriage, whereas in England the process was more gradual. In England after 1857 with the Matrimonial Causes Act and later Acts, marriage was removed from the control of ecclesiastical courts and adultery ceased to be a criminal offence. Marriage could be a civil condition and divorce became available in a way it had not been previously though its conditions still favoured men. Missions, particularly in Africa, even raised what is still the vexed issue of polygamy, since it was clearly practised by the patriarchs.

Thereafter in England there were two great changes affecting sexuality. One was the availability of techniques for deciding when and whether to have children, accepted by the Anglican Church in 1930. The other was the legislation of 1967 decriminalising homosexuality. By the twenty-first century homosexuals had been given equal rights to marriage, even in Ireland in 2015, and by a decision of the supreme Court of the USA in the same year. It was also evident from the demographic decline in Catholic countries that clerical attempts to control sexuality were largely ineffective. At the same time the status and independence of women gradually improved, especially under the impact of the two World Wars. By the late twentieth century most of the Protestant churches had accepted women as priests, pastors and ministers.

The Issues Raised by Sexuality

One of the reasons why sexuality cannot ever be innocent turns on the way it is linked with every other form of power, intimate, economic and political, including the aesthetic. That linkage between all the spheres subject to the Axial reserve about 'the world' is central to my argument in all my commentaries on the governing essay. The intersection of each and every sphere proposed by the accepted link between sex and violence is well founded. We have now to work it out.

A good place to start might be the madrigals of Gesualdo, a Renaissance prince who enforced his honour by cutting the throat of his unfaithful wife and having her lover butchered. The tortured dissonances of his music are expressionist depictions of the dynamic of sexual desire and desire for death and violence long before the advent of Expressionism.

Monteverdi did not write tortured music but his madrigals of Love and War explore the same dynamic, and notably in the case of *Il Combattimento do Tancredi e Clorinda* add the religious dimension explicitly to the mix. This is a particularly rich instance of the mutual suction of sex and violence, taken from Tasso's tale of Tancred, the Christian crusader knight and Clorinda the Saracen maiden in *Gerusalemme Liberata*. The story was used in several operatic libretti as well as in this *scena* from Monteverdi's eighth book of madrigals. The mutual sexual desire of the two crosses enemy, and religious, lines and is consummated in battle, with Clorinda, disguised in male armour, dying in single combat with Tancred but requesting baptism at his hands before she expires. The fusion between sex, violence and religion is exemplary.

Consider also the alternative Passion story, *Written on the Skin* (2012), a contemporary opera composed by George Benjamin to a libretto by Martin Crimp based on a troubadour's tale retold in Boccaccio's *Decameron* which might almost be derived from Gesualdo's life. An Angel comes to earth in Provence as a Boy because he is curious about what it is like to have a body. He is employed by a wealthy landowner, the Protector, to make and illuminate a book in his household. The Protector's wife, Agnes, watches the Boy at work and the two fall in love. When the Protector discovers the affair he kills the boy by cutting out his heart and feeding it forcibly to Agnes. She runs to the top of the house and commits suicide by throwing herself off the roof.

This Passion narrative unites all the key binaries: spiritual and embodied; heaven and earth; sexual love as possession by brute violence/sexual love as tender ecstatic connection. It illustrates two different forms of absorbing 'the Other', one through sexual congress and the merging of bodies, and the other an image of forcing a woman to ingest the rival's body in a black parody of the Eucharist. The story shows the Protector using sexuality as a weapon of power and dominance, and it shows Agnes finding in it liberation from that power and dominance. We have here a common pattern of interpersonal politics in which sexuality is centrally implicated, and one which underlines the intimate link between sexuality and violence as expressed in the conventional term 'crime of passion'. The very telling of the tale involves several art forms, music and poetry, and theatre as the natural habitat for expressions of the erotic and its ramifications. Another instructive example might be provided by Wagner's *Parsifal* where Kundry represents the principle of sexual gratification, Amfortas, the leader of the Knights of the Grail, is stricken with an unhealed sexual wound, and Parsifal represents the principle of moral and social innocence and purity. What Wagner's opera underscores is the way in which the sexual is so widely seen as the antithesis of the spiritual.

Interpersonal dynamics as set out in opera are not so very different from inter-tribal dynamics as set out and prescribed in the Torah. We can now turn to a much older paradigmatic story. The general principle of warfare as set out in Deuteronomy 20 is to approach a city and declare a reciprocal peace if the inhabitants are willing to submit as 'tributaries'. If the city refuses the Israelites are to besiege it and conquer it, killing all the males while, as for the rest – the women, children and cattle – these are theirs for eating and taking as 'the spoil of your enemies'. This murderous progress is often repeated with varying results as part of the covenant between the Lord and his people, if they obey his commandments. It was a bargain neither party kept, but it has remained notionally in place to this day.

As I have earlier indicated, William Blake would have called this ferocious projection of tribal fantasy 'Old Nobodaddy' and this non-entity continually asserts his malign presence in normative Scriptures. As we have seen, Islam finds 'the world' and social nature relatively unproblematic and is not much troubled by reservations in principle about sex and violence. When it comes to Islam, politicians are clear that no 'real' religion approves of violence because 'real' religion is by definition dedicated to the pursuit of peace. This surprising ability to define real religion over against other kinds has its uses. But the practices of the so-called Islamic State, or Isis, with regard to sex and violence can be defended from normative scripture quite effectively. After all it is a very poor exegete who cannot quote selectively from normative scriptures, whether the Koran or the Bible, to justify whatever frightfulness the *real-politik* of the moment demands, especially when the end in view is the eschatological dream of setting up the perfect state where Allah is obeyed to the letter.

Isis regularly beheads or crucifies its enemies and these automatically include all non-Muslims as well as Muslims who have other views about what Islam 'really' teaches. For Isis extreme terror is a weapon of war: so much for its attitude to violence. But it is abundantly clear that its attitude to violence is entirely of a piece with its attitude to women and sex. The two cannot be separated. It seems that the young women it entices to enjoy the aphrodisiac of violence are happy to see themselves as baby-machines to reproduce the perfect Islamic future, notably the next generation of warriors. As for the 'enemies' Isis captures, the men are murdered and the young women taken as sex slaves on a pattern graphically illustrated in the book of Deuteronomy.

From this it is not so great a leap to the Duke of Wellington as you might think. The Duke certainly abjured frightfulness as a weapon of war but in his sexual behaviour he was as 'innocent' as any pagan in classical times as described by Diarmaid MacCullough.[6] It was just that his wife paid the costs of his innocent adventures. Warring and whoring went together: once arrived in Paris as conqueror Wellington sought out the women who had previously enjoyed the attentions of Napoleon. The principle is of very wide application. If you can rape or impregnate the women of the enemy, whether in Europe or (say) Rwanda, you can occupy his ethnic base in the most intimate manner possible. In the Second World War all the Allied troops who entered defeated Germany behaved as the victorious German troops had done in the earlier phases of the conflict. Indeed the Russian troops were expressly told 'the German women are yours'. One needs to remember the etymology of rape and rapine. 'Rapio' means 'I take' in all the numerous meanings of the word.

Wars as a form of 'taking' are based on the violation of boundaries. But they are not the only way in which boundaries can be violated. Earlier we noted that extreme violence could be eschatologically motivated as part of the project of setting up the perfect society. This kind of society breaks all settled bounds, especially personal property and privacy. It is one of the paradoxes of Christian history that the sectarian urge to set up a perfect community is simultaneously associated with the principled withdrawal from every kind of violence *and* with the execution of violence on those who stand in the way of perfection. What characteristically happens is that at some stage in the process of setting up a revolutionary commune, the leader, maybe with the support of an inner group of associates, recommends a community of goods and of women. Extreme egalitarianism then mutates into a dictatorship where the leader exercises a monopoly over both the goods and the women. Mutations of this kind occur equally in politics and religion. Politics and religion are not the same but they are both as mythic as they are rational and they gain from being analysed together. Joseph Stalin and the charismatic leader of the Taiping Rebellion in China had much in common.

Here I am talking about a link between asceticism and an antinomian indifference to the rules governing ordinary humankind. Total moral discipline in the service of a great cause is a major weapon of war but it can break down into orgiastic behaviour. Cromwell's model army was served by antinomian chaplains. The Grande Armée was another hugely effective mass mobilisation of citizens behind a cause. But I am mainly interested here in a different link illustrating the intimate intersection of all the key spheres affected by a reserve about 'the world': the link between the erotic and the aesthetic.

6　In the three-part TV series mentioned earlier: *Sex and the Church*, BBC Two, May 2015.

My initial example happens to be the link between the erotic and the aesthetic among the Cistercians who had an objection to representation bordering on iconoclasm. The Cistercians built austerely because they objected to luxurious appointments in monasteries at the expense of Christ's poor. But this severity was itself aesthetically pleasing. They also illustrate the way affect becomes redirected among the great spiritual brotherhoods of the Middle Ages. They fed on the erotic imagery of the Song of Songs and St Bernard wrote sermons on the meaning of a text that in its original sense was an ecstatic celebration of human love. Once again we encounter the paradox of sublimity and humility in the context of the creaturely. In his commentary on the Song of Songs Bernard brings sublimity and humility together, celebrating earthly habitations that are also heavenly palaces. Transpositions of this kind occur again and again and identical tropes are found in the poetry of Pietism where the soul enters into intimate dialogue with its Lord.

Charles Wesley is the pre-eminent poet of erotic imagery in the service of devotion. People react to it subconsciously in an erotic as well as a devotional register. They seem to pass quite naturally from the erotic to the devotional mood. Perhaps the most famous example is 'Jesus, Lover of my soul/Let me to thy bosom fly .../Other refuge have I none/Hangs my helpless soul on Thee/ Leave, ah! leave me not alone/Still support and comfort me.' Such verse is, of course, part of the experiential appeal of Evangelicalism, particularly to women. Perhaps the most dramatic union of emotional violence and the erotic, which may be heterosexual or homosexual, occurs in the paintings of Caravaggio.

But maybe enough examples have been given to establish the likelihood of a strong connection between sex and violence. The key to understanding the consequences of the presence of a reserve towards the givens of our social nature and 'the grain' of 'the world' lies in the way all the spheres of human action are closely interconnected and flood into each other, from the economic and political to the erotic and the aesthetic. You cannot applaud Christianity as the religion you have (but do not believe in) as socially acceptable on account of its economic ethic and its apparent pacifism and dismiss its attitude to sexuality as an oddity that does not fit the overall progressive picture. We are not dealing with historical happenstance but with the pervasive influence of elective affinities and social logic, especially as they work themselves out with regard to sex and violence. It is no accident that Jesus nether fought nor married.

Fourth Commentary

On Peace and Violence

Theoretical Considerations

Throughout these commentaries I argue that the attitude to peace and violence is the key marker for understanding where any post-Axial faith stands. The Axial revolution radically reduces the diacritical markers to a strictly limited set. For my analytic purposes I begin here with a faith's attitude to violence, not with whether it believes in God. The kind of God worshipped by a given faith depends on that faith's attitude to violence. That implies, *incidentally*, that confronted by the monotheistic God of Islam I am a devout atheist. It is not remotely a question as to whether there is any evidence that such a God exists. After all, classical theology makes it very clear that God does not exist alongside other existences. The question that concerns me is the nature of God and whether he is worthy of worth-ship.

It may seem that here I have shifted from sociological analysis to a statement of belief, or rather of non-belief. On the contrary I am saying that *analytically* the question of God's existence is secondary to the attitude a faith takes to violence and that I *happen* not to believe in a God who simply reflects our social nature and the way 'the world' is with respect to violence as a weapon of domination. There is a total difference between a God, or gods, reflecting the way of the world with regard to violence, and a faith that seeks to transcend our social nature. Islam's God reflects the way of the world rather faithfully and to that extent is pre-Axial. Buddhism and Jainism seek to transcend 'the world' and our social nature by denying its reality and making the existence of gods or God secondary. The oddity of Christianity is both to accept the reality of the world as God's creation and to seek to transcend it with the vision of the rule of God.

In my book on *Pacifism* I expressed the matter rather differently. I simply placed the main world faiths in a limited logical set based on whether 'the world' was accepted in principle as real and on whether 'the world' understood as our 'social nature' was seen as in need of transformation. Islam stood out as a faith that accepted the world as it is and was therefore incapable of generating a movement opposed to the use of force. Perhaps wisely, I avoided any reference to what I personally might believe or disbelieve, and that was partly because faith is not at all a matter of belief but the embrace of a Way. Evidence is hardly crucial to questions about the relation of saving grace to the resistances of our social nature, though one might note in favour of Augustine over against Pelagius that these resistances are not easily rooted out. Empirically sin appears endemic and recalcitrant. In the same way one might note that the evidence for God's providential care for his people or for any other category of his creatures is not noticeably above random. Tennyson, in his great threnody *In Memoriam*, was quite right to comment that God was not even 'careful of the type'.[1]

Religious affirmations live and move within ways of 'being in the world' to which empirical arguments are otiose. There is something to be said for indicating why religious affirmations are not excluded by scientific evidence, but beyond that, the language of faith has nothing in common with propositional language or scientific analysis. All our life-choices belong to the category of existence and express the freedom of the spirit within definable limiting parameters and are therefore beyond empirical adjudication, without contradicting it. They are subject to costs and benefits following a moral calculus that includes all the various discourses of tragedy. They have nothing in common with superstition, because superstition is a matter of mistaken empirical causation not of existential choice.

As I have suggested throughout these commentaries, religious affirmations are forms of symbolic logic springing from fundamental attitudes to 'the world'. Think only of the hymns of Thomas Aquinas about the divinity latent in 'figures' within bread and wine and it is just obvious that apprehensions of this kind are not subject to empirical adjudication. The Bible contains nothing beyond some scattered hints about number and line in the Wisdom literature that can be reduced to propositions. The word 'Glory', for example, is simultaneously an ascription and an ecstatic response, but it is not informative. Science has nothing to say about faith, hope and love, or about the priority of love. Love is like glory: part of the very specific language of Christianity. It overlaps other human languages but its meanings and grammar are specific and derive from an attitude towards 'the world'.

And that attitude turns on an approach to violence. If one pauses only for a moment to consider what is involved in economic and political power, as well as in the exercise of power in our most intimate relations, including erotic power, the role of violence is very clear. This is not to deny that human beings can cooperate

---

[1]   Tennyson's poem was written between 1833 and 1850. This particular quotation comes from sections xv-xvi and there are more hopeful attitudes expressed in section cxxiv. Tennyson, *Selected Poems*, p. 140.

to pursue common ends, or to deny that they can feel love and sympathy one for another. We can act harmoniously and we can seek the resolution of disputes, but the human drama is kept 'in play' by discord and disharmony. Our economic, political and familial arrangements and negotiations contain an ineluctable element of violence. Some forms of power are so overwhelming that the use of physical violence is rendered unnecessary. The rulers can plausibly declare 'peace where there is no peace'. The covert threat of violence is enough. That is what is meant by hegemony, whether we are talking about imperialism or the relations of the sexes in Strindberg's *The Father* or *Miss Julie*. In this perspective nothing, least of all sex, is free of coercion. In the very specific language of Christianity everything partakes of the nature of sin. Our projects are throughout subject to corruption.

If it is the oddity of Christianity to both accept 'the world' or 'the creation' as in principle good but in need of redemption at very great cost, it is also the oddity of Christianity to acknowledge the ubiquity of sin and corruption and yet to envisage *metanoia* and transformation. This acknowledgement is already present in Judaism in spite of a less acute angle of transcendence: the psalmist declares that *The earth shall be full of the knowledge of the Lord as the waters cover the sea*. In Christianity it is acknowledged by the announcement of the coming kingdom in the fourth chapter of St Luke's Gospel, roughly quoting Isaiah 61: '*The Spirit of the Lord is upon* me because he has anointed me to preach the gospel to the poor, he has sent *me to heal the brokenhearted, to preach deliverance to the captives and recovery of sight to the blind, to set at liberty them that are bruised*'. But the problem that then arises is the cost of redemption because the redemptive encounter with violence will involve exemplary violence inflicted on the body of the redeemer. The redeemer absorbs the cost in his own body and by way of a subjection to the 'powers' of this world through death on the cross, something that Islam considers impairs the glory of God rather than providing its most profound expression.

Our concern here is with the emergence of a principled rejection of violence and coercion within religious languages embodying an acute angle of transcendence. Such a rejection could hardly be more radical because psychologically our 'nature' is based on fight and flight, and sociologically our nature is based on the solidarity of 'Us' set against the solidarity of 'Them'. What binds us together sets us apart. The dynamics of cooperation and conflict are inherently bound up with the dynamics of mobilisation and pre-emption as set out in the classical accounts of Thucydides and Josephus, let alone in the 'realist' school of international relations. This brings us immediately back to the contrast set out in the governing essay between a Niebuhrian view of Christianity as against the grain of 'the world', and pacifist views that suppose the principled rejection of violence and coercion corresponds to the way the social world could work if only we had sufficient faith.

The problem here is not merely that faith needs to stretch itself beyond any plausible limit but that 'we' are never united in pursuing pacifism to the point where the good effects optimistically anticipated come to fruition, given that 'we', considered as an ordinary viable social unit, are never likely to be united in pursuit of dangerous utopian projects. The argument has to be that somebody needs to initiate a virtuous circle and hope that this good example will so prevail on human hardness of heart that potential enemies come to realise how much superior peace is to war.

However, the virtuous circle never has a chance to be simultaneously implemented on all sides, and that means that 'we' have to withdraw from ordinary society into a sectarian enclave of those who can agree among themselves. We are back immediately to the basic sociological distinction between a 'church' as an institution 'in the mixture' seeking viable compromises with the world and with the regime of violence, and the sect as an enclave of the like-minded bound together by a non-coercive consensus against the dynamics of pre-emptive mobilisation. This bifurcation within Christianity derives directly from the acute angle of transcendence, and the doctrine of the just war is the characteristic response of ecclesiastical institutions embedded in society as it is and striving to ameliorate and negotiate the tension between 'the kingdom' and 'the world'. If there were no such tension there would be no need to expend so much intellectual energy justifying what just comes naturally.

The History of the Tension between Kingdom and World, Sect and Church

We have now to trace the history of that tension in Christian societies up to the present day. Perhaps the best place to begin is Isaiah's vision of a peaceable kingdom set up on a holy mountain where man and beast live together in harmony. The lion and the lamb lie down together and the child plays on the hole of the asp. This is not the only vision of a peaceable kingdom in the Hebrew Scriptures. Joel and Micah cherish similar anticipations. The context seems to be eschatological and embedded in the final war when the Lord puts the enemies of Israel to flight or maybe establishes peace between the warring nations by his power and might. Paul in his epistle to the Corinthians 12:10 spiritualises the war of the Christian against sin, but, as we have argued elsewhere, spiritual warfare easily mutates back to physical warfare under the pressure of events. Life as envisaged on the holy mountain that rises in the latter days simultaneously cancels Darwin on the struggle for survival in nature and Thucydides on the dynamics of war-making.

Here we have a pattern that frequently reappears: eschatology, the anticipated rule of God and a last battle finally to establish peace. Clearly the pattern is not restricted to religious conceptions. It reappears in nineteenth-century Liberal idealism and finds exemplary expression in the urge to fight the good fight in order to win 'the war to end war'. Satan has been finally identified as the Enemy and once the forces of the alien have been destroyed peace will be established to the furthest ends of the earth.

So how do we bridge the gap between the image of the holy mountain two and a half millennia ago in the Axial Age and the dilemmas of contemporary politics in the twenty-first century? It is not at all accidental that the patterns and dilemmas that exercise us now are the same patterns and moral dilemmas that exercised people then. We and they are moral contemporaries because the problematic of 'kingdom' and 'world' as we and they understand it stems from an identical religious source established in our consciousness by a shared Scripture. We feel the need to apologise for acts of violence committed against others because we have failed by our own standards, but not by theirs. By their standards there is no radical disjunction between what they did do and what they ought to have done. It is neither a matter of credit nor of discredit. The Turks will refuse to acknowledge the Armenian genocide of 1915 not because they are merely brazen but because apology is not embedded in their vocabulary of motives. Of course, there are Turks who acknowledge the genocide: I am talking about the absence of anything remotely resembling public apology by the state or its representatives. In a very vigorous discussion in which I participated in Istanbul in 2005, Armenia only emerged in the context of a speech by a Kurd, who saw parallels with the oppression of Kurds, though Kurds had earlier cooperated with the Ottomans in the (equally unacknowledged) Assyrian genocide.

Axial civilisations embody angles of transcendence that generate visions of a kingdom of peace and righteousness. A restored world can either be created by violence or it may lie hidden in the womb of time. After the Jews had tried to 'restore the kingdom' by violence the rabbis of the second century bc decided it would be better to wait in patience. Josephus describes the political agitation of those Jews of New Testament times who brought about the catastrophic destruction of the temple and confirmed Christians in their belief in a kingdom 'not of this world'. One recollects here the maybe retrospective and post-ad 70 discourse of Jesus in Mark 13 about the illusory solidity of the temple. One also recollects the verses in Luke 22:35-8 where Jesus appears to raise the option of taking the sword only to dismiss it with the words 'It is enough'. This is the oscillation we observe in many other contexts, beginning with the holy mountain of Isaiah between peaceable waiting for the great and terrible Day of the Lord and becoming active agents of its advent.

Christianity emerged on the despised Galilean margin of a marginal people on the eastern frontiers of the Roman Empire. Constantine adopted the cross as a symbol guaranteeing victory: *in hoc signum vincit*. While retaining his own devotion to the sun god he ordered the cross to be placed on the shields of his army. It was at that point that Christianity bifurcated into the principled non-violence of the powerless and the exigencies of power as expressed in a *partially* renewed relation between faith and the powers of the cosmos. That bifurcation has constantly reappeared in monasticism, the Lollard movement and the Radical Reformation. There is a clear relationship between the political realism of the powerful allied to the 'territorial imperative' of violence, and the political idealism of the powerless allied to the perspectives available to members of a dispersed voluntary association.

The history of the Quakers as a self-selected and dispersed group with enormous international influence for liberal causes and above all for peace is paradigmatic. Quakers were part of the eschatological ferment that gripped England during the Civil War between 1642 and 1660. They were ejected from the Parliamentary forces not on account of any objection to fighting but because they were egalitarian radicals who refused 'hat honour'. In the same way they objected to churches as mere 'steeple houses' with pulpits occupied by 'professors' of the word rather than doers of the word. In what was presumably a conscious recreation of Isaiah's proclamation of the peaceable holy mountain, the Quaker leader, George Fox, ascended Pendle Hill in Lancashire to proclaim the Day of the Lord.

But the Quaker embrace of principled pacifism only emerged after the revolution had finally failed. It was then that the followers of George Fox declared they would fight neither for the kingdoms of this world nor for the kingdom of Christ. They represented a shift from outward to inward revolution and exemplified the oscillation over the previous two millennia since Isaiah between a new spiritual order achieved within and the kingdom of God actively set up on earth. The same sequence occurred among the radical sectarians of Münster in the 1530s. The Quakers emerged in the 1660s as a reorganised sect, sometimes drawn from militant groups like the Fifth Monarchy Men. They became a capsule of revolutionary potentials for peace and other causes protected within the strong boundaries of endogamy. In a similar way the Mennonites emerged from the extraordinary cauldron of revolution in Münster.

Moreover, the oscillation between lying low as 'the quiet in the land' and revolutionary activism occurred all over Europe on the margins of the Radical Reformation. These oscillations were associated with other and often quite rapid shifts between total transcendence and total immanence, and between moral perfectionism and antinomian moral licence of the kind attacked by Paul in Romans 6 among those 'who sinned the more that grace might abound the more'. That is how it could come about that the Puritan soldiery could cry with no sense of impropriety 'Jesus, and no quarter'.

Liberal internationalism appears to be a very different ideological formation rooted in the Enlightenment assumption that social problems like war could be solved by human agency, but there are powerful analogies between the problems and expectations of eschatological hope within a religious frame and expectations of the efficacy of secular reason to inaugurate a new world order within what looks like a secular frame: progress plays the role of the hoped for *eschaton*. Of course, humankind is motivated by interests and these might easily give rise to conflicts needing to be resolved by force, except that commercial capitalism and the exchange of goods ensured an international community of interest rather like the operation of the hidden hand in the economy. What Liberals initially had in common, alongside the happy operation of shared interest, was a belief in the potency of moral motives and the power of appeals to morality. Both these features of Liberal ideology were mistaken. Interests clash at the most fundamental level and politics resist moralisation. In the course of the nineteenth and early twentieth century, reality broke in, to the extent that a later generation of Liberals moved closer to an economic analysis of the causes of war generated by the incoherence of the capitalist system. Norman Angell was famous for exposing what he regarded as the irrationality of war, whereas Noel Brailsford expounded the role of economic motives for war. Brailsford also made the important point that a fundamental opposition to war had usually taken root among individuals whose primary concern was personal righteousness. As I shall argue below the question of personal righteousness provides a major clue to understanding Liberal pacifism.

One major consequence of a belief in the ultimate coincidence of interests and the potential for moralisation was a faith in the efficacy of efforts to achieve peace.[2] This belief in the viability of efforts to achieve peace and in the importance of conscience was not at all identical with strict pacifism as embraced

---

[2]   A nuanced account of these issues is provided in chapter 3 (pp. 64–115) of Hans Joas and Wolfgang Knöbl, *War in Social Thought: Hobbes to the Present*, Princeton: Princeton University Press, 2013. Ultimately Marxism shared in liberal optimism in spite of its seeming commitment to realism.

by sectarians like the Quakers. Nevertheless, Liberals and principled sectarians could work together for common causes, for example in the Peace Societies that emerged in the wake of the Napoleonic wars, especially in America and Britain. What followed was a remarkably peaceful period in European politics, except that in the latter part of the nineteenth century Germany increasingly adhered to an expansionist policy based on *real-politik* that upset the balance of power and encouraged the formation of alliances to restore the disturbed balance. Whichever set of alliances was ultimately to blame for what became a race to secure a balance of countervailing power hardly matters here. The vicious rather than the virtuous spiral was all too clearly the operative factor, and it became unpleasantly clear that international affairs were ordered according to the classic dynamics of pre-emption and the solidarity of one alliance against the other.

To some extent the encounter with reality could be avoided on account of the imperialist character of the wars which Britain in particular waged in the nineteenth century. A *real-politik* based on the imperatives of far-flung empire, whether in the Crimea or South Africa, was vulnerable to a vigorous moral critique such as the Quaker Liberal John Bright pursued with regard to the rationale of the Crimea War and what he saw as the criminal wastefulness of its prosecution. In other words, the moral vulnerability of these imperialist wars was such that it was not necessary to put into question the viability of Liberal 'pacificism' faced with choices between war and effective capitulation to the threat of war. The decent prejudice in favour of peace was not faced with ultimate choices and was protected in Britain and America by preponderant power and a degree of geographical isolation. There was no either/or. Morality was affordable, at least for the time being. There were even middle-class progressives who believed it was possible for Britain to play a decisive role in international affairs while avoiding military preparations and the moral entanglements of alliances and this form of belief in the force of moral example unsupported by military capacity has never disappeared.

Meanwhile foreign policy and international relations constituted an arena in which hitherto good men and true were mysteriously led astray, as Tony Blair was suborned by America decades later in the matter of the Iraq war. There was a search for culprits and the hidden sources of malignity, such as the practice of secret diplomacy, or the influence of the armament manufacturers, or (on the left) governments considered as mere executive committees of the ruling class and its economic interests. Things were otherwise where socialism was embraced in what Sydney and Beatrice Webb called the 'new civilisation' of Soviet Russia. It took decades of evidence about the real motives governing Russian foreign policy for this mythic hope to evaporate. The hope that somewhere other than in the corrupt capitalist West the sacred causes of peace and fraternity might be successfully pursued defied evidence among the most sophisticated members of the western intelligentsia. Utopian illusion is no monopoly of the ignorant: on the contrary.

Here we encounter the nemesis of an optimistic rationalism deriving from the Enlightenment and hopes of a perpetual peace. These combined with optimistic Christian derivatives appealing to the true meaning of the Kingdom of God rooted in the Sermon on the Mount and generalised invocations of the Fatherhood of God and the Brotherhood of Man. Insofar as true Christianity was identified with this selective reading of the New Testament it could be accorded some modest approbation well short of commitment.

We are dealing here with a bourgeois faith in reason utterly immune to evidence which focused its moral passion and sense of righteousness on foreign policy. Issues of war and peace emotionally dominated individualistic middle-class political morality. In this the Labour Party, attracting supporters imbued either with Protestant Dissent or rationalist utopianism, reproduced the attitudes previously associated with Liberal laissez-faire. There were no ineluctable choices where all the available options might trail tragic consequences. Every problem was soluble.

Earlier I suggested that the structural problems blocking the inauguration of the kingdom of God on earth were recapitulated in the problems facing the establishment of a new world order and what Immanuel Kant and the Abbé de Saint-Pierre hoped for by way of 'perpetual peace'. Liberalism like Christianity is against the grain of the world. We smile at the man bearing a placard warning us to flee the wrath to come, but eschatology, in the form of deepening crises and the last battle, looms over Jewish and Christian civilisation from its inception in Isaiah to the present day; nor is it absent from Islamic civilisation or Pure Land Buddhism. Of course, as inheritors of the search for correlations and causes we have to enquire systematically about the factors bearing on the incidence of violence, for example we have to ask what has activated the struggle between Shia and Sunni in the Middle East and how far we are dealing with a naked power struggle between Iran and Saudi Arabia. But the structural problem does not dissolve at the touch of scientific analysis.

Liberal internationalists are and have been peculiarly inclined to embrace wars with the moral aim of ending war and establishing perpetual peace. That means they reject war in its everyday form as the instrument of the contingent twists and turns of national interest carried out by military professionals. Instead they enthusiastically pursue war as a crusade. That means that they reject the analysis of the limits on the moralisation of relations between nations proposed by Reinhold Niebuhr. Liberals hold to a set of internally coherent principles such as Hobhouse's belief in the common good or T.H. Green's faith in conscience, but the Liberal view of the scope for righteousness is misled by myth.[3] Liberals act as though motivated by an implicit eschatology of the brighter future just behind the obstructive veil of the moment, not by a negotiation of means and ends that may, with a good following wind, turn out marginally better than the alternatives. They are inhabitants of the end-times in which the issues that will govern human destiny are finally to be joined.

Meanwhile there are pure lands elsewhere which truly embody the last and best hopes of humankind. Political life must be moralised and guided by the imperatives of righteousness rather than those of power, else the righteous would prefer to be unblemished moral critics rather than compromised participants. Commentary is easier than action. In common with the sects of the Radical Reformation they may oscillate between making love and making war, between imitating the action of the panther and cooing like the holy dove. There are no tragic choices where all the options trail a potential for disaster. Human beings cannot but follow the light once it has been revealed to them by the children of the light. The world is divided into those of goodwill and those of ill-will. And it is an article of faith that the children of darkness will not in the end prevail.

---

[3]   L.T. Hobhouse, *The Rational Good*, New York: Henry Holt, 1921; Melvin Richter, *The Politics of Conscience: T.H. Green and his Age*, Cambridge, MA: Harvard University Press, 1954.

On the Return of the Liturgical in Modernist Music and Poetry and the Reconciliation Achieved by Liturgical Poetry and Music

My discussion of the return of the liturgical with the advent of modernism, and maybe also with the advent of modernity, seeks to understand the resilience of Christianity in music and poetry, especially in the modern period roughly coextensive with the twentieth century. The twentieth century has been characterised as a secular age where immanence rather than transcendence can be taken for granted, so a palpable interest in sacred music originally composed for the liturgy has considerable interest. It is therefore an implicit critique of the kind of secularisation theory that treats the transition from the religious to the secular as unilinear. As I, and others, have argued, the process is not unilinear, and the religious and the secular are not so easily distinguished, the one from the other. Given the immensity of the subject I am restricting myself to western music and in poetry my references are mainly restricted to English.

There is a wider context to my argument than pointing out, as I have done several times previously, that the history of music and poetry does not support a straightforward and unilinear understanding of secularisation. I am concerned with liturgy, and in particular Christian liturgy, as a fundamental form of collective, impersonal and minutely choreographed human action. Its collective and impersonal form is crucial. It predates by millennia its individual actors and invites them simply to play a predetermined role within the ensemble of roles and to do so in a manner that holds idiosyncrasy and personality strictly in check. Even the sermon as a spoken form within the context of liturgy depends on the individual suppressing quotidian opinions about this or that in order to elucidate readings appropriate to a particular point in the liturgical cycle from the perspective of a given tradition.

In the account of musical history that I attempt here I identify various historical phases up to 'the break' that begins to occur in the latter half of the

eighteenth century and comes to a revolutionary climax with the advent of
Romanticism in the years from 1780 to 1820. Humanity at large or the specific
claims of nationalism and political ideology displace the Church, and individual
apprehensions of transcendence displace collective liturgical participation.
Christians like Anton Bruckner (or in poetry Gerard Manley Hopkins) become
explicit about their commitments rather than conforming, like Josquin or
Monteverdi, or Bach and Handel, to the 'taken for granted'. Bach and Handel
did not live in particularly religious environments but their very different kinds
of genuine devotion were expressed in taken for granted forms. I am arguing here
that after the Romantic period, lasting on an extended definition, up the early
twentieth century, collective liturgical action returned centre-stage. It did so in
very unexpected 'secular' environments, as though these environments, in Russia
(say) or Britain or France, threw into high relief the necessity of liturgy, and
specifically the necessity of Christian liturgy. Christian liturgy acknowledges
the ubiquity of moral ruin in a landscape of abject brokenness, and it seeks
redemption and reconciliation through the restoration of full communion. It
therefore fits the overall argument about the brokenness of the world and the
need for redemption that informs these various commentaries.

My emphasis is on music with occasional excursions into poetry.[1] I am
assuming that music and poetry are closely related languages that have an affinity
with the language of Christianity. Poetry rests on metaphor and metaphor
illuminates reality from a perspective that exploits similarity and difference.[2]
Music is a vehicle to transcendence that goes beyond even the most articulate
speech. Whereas speech is restricted by the grammar of consequences, so that if
this is the case then that normally follows, music is as free as flying. Its grammar is
internal to itself. I am suggesting that Christianity, poetry and music are related
languages that in different ways transform the given and set 'the world' in the
light of transcendence.

I begin with a brief examination of the main phases of music which are, as
it happens, also closely related to the main phases of poetry. Restricting myself
to western art music there are several clearly distinguished phases. There is the
period up to roughly 1200, even though the changes that occurred then go back
centuries earlier to experiments in the monastery of St Gall. Prior to 1200 the

---

[1]   I gave up my initial and unworkable idea of discussing in some detail poets I knew
personally with a clear interest in liturgy, like Donald Davie, Geoffrey Hill, Charles Sisson
and Simon Jarvis, together with others like (say) Denise Levertov and Michael Symonds
Roberts. This task is for a literary critic with a knowledge of theology. I did not find the
eclectic spirituality of W.B. Yeats relevant to my argument.

[2]   Denis Donoghue, *Metaphor*, Cambridge, MA: Harvard University Press, 2014.

dominant form of music was plainchant, a liturgical music which may well have had major origins in the East, for example, the music of the synagogue. Music entered a revolutionary phase in the thirteenth century with the invention of polyphony. The invention of polyphony occurred in Paris and is associated with the rather shadowy figures of Machaut and Pérotin, and it ran roughly parallel with the rise of Gothic architecture in Paris and the associated metaphysics of light as envisaged by the Abbott Suger of Saint Denis. Polyphony dominated music for the next four hundred years up to 1600, when it was superseded by the creation in Italy of the Baroque style, which lasted up to about 1750. Whereas in the polyphonic period there was some differentiation of sacred vocal and secular vocal music, the Baroque saw the emergence of highly expressive secular opera based on classical themes, emphasising words and seeking harmonic tension and stylised 'affect'. Similar kinds of 'affect' were pursued by instrumental music for keyboard and for strings, notably orchestral suites and *concerti grossi*. The main sources of patronage in the Baroque era remained the Church and the Court, and the theory of music remained within a modified Platonic framework that stressed the moral and metaphysical nature of music. The poetry of John Dryden written at the end of the seventeenth century in praise of music still retains an explicit metaphysical framework rather than the generalised invocation of elevated feelings popular in the nineteenth century.

This relative stability achieved by the Baroque came to an end in the eighteenth century, though one must be careful about equating the Baroque in music with the Baroque in architecture, and sensitive to different rates of change in music and intellectual enquiry, including poetry. The two greatest masters of the Baroque, Bach and Handel, remained within the ambit of Christianity up to around 1750, whereas a poem like Dryden's *Religio Laici* (1682) seems very much a rearguard action in the face of what Hazard has called the crisis in European consciousness from 1680 to 1715.[3] Handel was, of course, above all a composer of opera to heroic renaissance themes up to roughly 1740, and his English mutation of the kind of oratorio originally invented in Italy appealed to a new lay middle class. It later became a mainstay of mass Protestant choral music and has been falsely blamed for the inanition of English music. Nevertheless the association of music with religion was going through a major transformation that became obvious in the later eighteenth century with the pre-classics like C.P.E. Bach, and Haydn wrote symphonies and chamber music that exhibited a new sense of irony and reflected the emotions of *Sturm und Drang*. Storm

---

[3]   Paul Hazard, *The European Mind: The Critical Years*, trans. J. Lewis May, New Haven: Yale University Press, 1953.

and stress broke out in the revolutionary transformations of Romanticism between 1780 and 1820. What happened between Mozart in the 1780s, as the great composer of dramatic music with subversive political implications, and Beethoven in the early 1800s was as revolutionary in music as it was politically in Europe with the advent of the French Revolution. If one wanted to pinpoint that revolutionary transition to Romanticism one could hardly do better than the second movement of the piano trio, opus 72, number 1, known as 'The Ghost', because Beethoven may have been using material suggested by a projected work on Shakespeare's *Macbeth*.

One way of introducing these changes might be through changing visions of Nature. Handel's setting of Milton's *L'Allegro* evoked the natural world of a rather bucolic English countryside but it also hinted in a sequel on 'Moderation' loosely based on Shakespeare at a rational understanding of the world where the 'fumes of fancy' were dispersed by 'intellectual day'. This approach paralleled the new attitude to Nature expressed by Joseph Addison for whom the Newtonian universe was fully established yet remained the handiwork of the creator. Two poets whose work was set by major musicians indicate the change of tone. Barthold Brockes was a Pietist but in his poetry of the early eighteenth century, set by Handel, there is no trace of Pietism, only a frank enjoyment of rushing streams and flaming roses, as part of the divine creation, and providing solace for the appreciative soul. James Thomson was nurtured in Calvinism but in his very widely influential poem *The Seasons* (1730), set by Haydn in 1801, he simply celebrates the changing countryside, for example in his tone painting of a bountiful harvest. Haydn's *The Creation*, composed in 1798, leaves behind the framework of redemption to celebrate the magnificent work of the creator like the writer of Psalm 104. The early years of the 1800s bring a further revolution in attitudes of Nature. Beethoven's sixth symphony (1808) marks the change. For Beethoven the woods are a holy of holies, and Nature a reposeful school of the heart that reflects our deepest desires. Schubert also apostrophised Nature, the sun, flora and fauna, and expressed a vision of landscape that contrasted with the mechanistic attitude promoted by Cartesianism. Schubert's *Wanderer* in the natural world was pursued by yearning and melancholy. But more than that, Ian Bostridge in his *Schubert's Winter Journey: Anatomy of an Obsession*[4] treats the work as canonical, ineffable and transcendent in the same way as the Bach Passions.

---

[4]   Ian Bostridge, *Schubert's Winter Journey: Anatomy of an Obsession*, London: Faber & Faber, 2015.

Haydn, Beethoven and Schubert bring us to Vienna, the epicentre of musical revolution. First, however, we should notice, in London as well as Vienna, a new interest in the 'antique' music of the past and the incipient formation of a musical canon, beginning with Handel, the first composer to be memorialised in his own lifetime. The creation of a canon suggests how music might be in process of becoming a power analogous to religion rather than the role of the 'handmaid' of faith envisaged by Luther. The very word 'classical' applied to music dates from the mid-nineteenth century.

That shift towards music as an independent source of transcendence was reinforced by a new and serious audience in the concert hall and festival venue, rather than Court and Church, that focused on the large-scale instrumental music of symphony, sonata and concerto. That shift was also signalled in the intimate domestic sphere of chamber music and, as already indicated, in the emergence of *lieder* responding to German Romantic poetry. Perhaps chamber music as the benison of transcendence in the domestic sphere is most perfectly represented by Mozart's six string quartets of the mid-1780s dedicated to Haydn, and in the quartets following them. Beethoven picked up the tradition through remarkable string trios which led in roughly 1800 to his Op. 18 set of six string quartets: trenchant, intense, impatient and programmatic – a new century and a new world.

The nineteenth century was the age of the piano in the drawing room and the virtuoso performer in the concert hall, above all Franz Liszt, and of grand-evocative gestures on the themes of lost love, destiny and death. Alfred Brendel has analysed the very different ways in which the middle to late works of Schubert and Beethoven explored the inner world in depth, often with a sense of profound tragedy.[5] Both composers were opposed to the conservative politics of Vienna, and Beethoven in particular became a ubiquitous icon of the rebellious genius who, in works like *Fidelio* and the *Eroica Symphony* (1804–5) and the *Choral Symphony* (1822–4), had welcomed the onset of a new age of revolution, political liberation and of Humanity standing joyfully before God. The *Missa Solemnis* of Beethoven and the final E flat mass of Schubert step outside the liturgy of the church to address humanity directly. In their monumentality they mark the conclusion of an era of classical mass settings by Haydn and Mozart. However much animated by genuine piety, these settings are in scale, temper and ceremonial grandeur outside the normal framework of the liturgy. They require musical resources way beyond the local church choir.

Here we need to give some account of the repertoire of feeling in Romanticism from Schubert and Beethoven, Schumann and Mendelssohn

---

[5]   In a set of DVD recordings of Schubert with associated commentaries.

onwards. We also need to trace a shift from an assumption of Christian belief as part of what may be socially taken for granted to a more personal piety that may include agnosticism. Mendelssohn was genuinely pious and recouped a Jewish heritage within a Christian frame but in great geniuses like Beethoven and Goethe religious feeling becomes idiosyncratic and world views are personally constructed. The supreme musical expressions of this might be the Adagio of Schubert's late Quintet and Beethoven's *Heiliger Dankgesang*.

With regard to the Romantic repertoire of feeling one finds a window onto it in the paintings of Caspar David Friedrich in Germany and Samuel Palmer and John Constable in England. In Caspar David Friedrich one has Humanity outlined in solitary grandeur against the vast backdrop of Nature, and the Church, especially the multivalent sign of the cross, is a major part of the ensemble of Nature. For Friedrich as a Lutheran the cross 'veers strangely between physical presence and dream-like vision, between a prop in the landscape and a unique vision of God'.[6]

In poetry, for example in Wordsworth and Coleridge, one has variable apprehensions of the divine presence in Nature, while in music there is a more generalised awareness of the place of the Gothic building in iconic landscapes, for example Cologne Cathedral juxtaposed to the flowing Rhine in a song by Robert Schumann. The invocation of the Middle Ages in Romanticism creates a diffusely Catholic atmosphere which is supplemented by an invocation of the spirit of the folk. The German *lied* celebrates balladry, chivalry, chiming towers, old pictures, the grotesque and the teeming life of ancient cities like Venice. For more explicitly Christian images of incarnation and redemption one has to turn to the vocal music of Hugo Wolf in the 'spiritual' songs within the *Spanisches Liederbuch* (1891).

In the latter part of the nineteenth century religion is a personal matter which includes explicit agnosticism. Explicit agnosticism in Brahms is partnered by explicit Catholicism in Bruckner and Liszt and there is no reason to doubt Liszt's personal devotion on account of his uniquely flamboyant lifestyle. Both Brahms and Mahler are interesting. Brahms comes from a northern Protestant background and he combines his explicit agnosticism with a deeply felt exploration of religious themes, for example in his German *Requiem*, for which he personally selected the biblical texts, and in his *Four Serious Songs*. Mahler was an assimilated Jew, who converted to Christianity and focused in

---

    6   Johannes Grave, 'Under the Sign of the Cross: The Religious Picture', in Johannes Grave, *Caspar David Friedrich*, London, New York and Munich: Prestel, 2012, pp. 91–109, at p. 103.

his intertwined songs and symphonies on death, destiny and Resurrection and also invoked the Spirit and the cosmic. The range of themes was now reaching beyond Europe: Mahler's *Das Lied von der Erde* (c.1909) set Chinese poetry. In Mahler and in the early Schönberg, for example the pantheistic *Gurrelider*, the tonal system was breaking down in a mood of elegiac richness still present in Richard Strauss's *Four Last Songs* (1948). In Strauss the religious impulse was barely present at all.

We turn now from the Austro-German trajectory to a comparison between changes in France and Britain. The two countries are sharply contrasted in their musical and religious histories along lines suggested by the historian Élie Halévy. France was the epicentre of the revolutionary impulse from the 1790s on and therefore of singing groups with repertoires and sentiments contrasted in their political zeal with the pious choral traditions of Britain. France was also an epicentre of a nationalism that through the conquests of Napoleon stirred up nationalism all over Europe, for example in Germany and Russia. Berlioz gave up the fervent Catholicism of his youth but nevertheless wrote monumental works like the *Te Deum* and the *Grande Messe des Morts* (1837), composed for a great national occasion in memory of those who died in the revolution of 1830. The Franco-Polish composer Chopin also wrote music suffused with national sentiment but with no more reference to religion than you might find in the operas of Bizet. Though the mid-to-late nineteenth century saw a partial recovery of Catholicism, church music often sounded operatic. As for opera itself, religion often figured as integral to the drama, as for example in Massenet's far-from-biblical *Hérodiade* (1881), or made a broader political point as in Halévy's *La Juive* (1835) and Meyerbeer's *Les Huguenots* (1836), dedicated to religious tolerance. At the same time there was an important school of sacred music associated with the Franco-Belgian tradition of organ music. In Belgium César Franck wrote for the organ and composed *Les Béatitudes*, and in France Gabriel Fauré wrote a requiem mass that has become a major part of the choral repertory.

In general late nineteenth-century and early twentieth-century French music made only modest references to religion: Ravel was Jewish and Debussy was a semi-pagan Nature mystic who confined himself to setting *The Martydom of Saint Sebastian* to a text by D'Annunzio. Both Ravel and Debussy (for example in the *Préludes* of Book 1 of 1910) were pioneers of musical modernism in their treatment of tonality. If one wants some sense of the trajectory of French music it is best traced in French *mélodie* from Berlioz in the 1830s to Poulenc a century or so later. French song is suffused with images of cemeteries, tombs, spectres, perfumes, clouds, tresses, flutes, satyrs and fauns, and with hints of oriental exoticism. It luxuriates and sometimes evokes the atmosphere of the salon and the café.

The British, more particularly the English trajectory, was markedly different, in large part because of the influence of Evangelicalism and the way emotional piety channelled change into evolutionary reform rather than revolution. Opera, with its louche traditions, made little headway in England apart from the Savoy operettas associated with the light music of Arthur Sullivan. Oratorio dominated, especially the masterpieces of Handel, Haydn and Mendelssohn, and Mendelssohn set the tone of a kind of religious sentiment that suffused the market for anthems and cantatas, especially in the music for the great choral festivals. The Victorian hymn was represented by the publication in the 1860s and 1870s of *Hymns Ancient and Modern*. Works like Charles Gounod's *Mors et Vita* and *The Redemption* were performed at the Birmingham Festival and easier works like Stainer's *Crucifixion* (1887) became part of the annual cycle. The hymn had by this time long displaced the metrical psalm and Evangelicalism ran in parallel with German pietism to feed into the democratic musical traditions of America in revivalist choruses and Gospel music. In the nineteenth century musicians included fiddlers, virtuosi and songbirds but with industrial society and mass communication music became a profession with colleges and conservatoires and an increasing historical self-consciousness that fed the retrieval of so-called 'early music' and made all the phases of musical development available to contemporary taste. Plainsong and polyphony might provide up-to-date spiritual mood music like the undulations of the ocean.

There was major change under way about 1870, musically, politically and socially. Britain was the first industrial and urban society but the revival of music took a surprisingly religious and even rural colouring. In Edward Elgar Britain had a major composer for the first time since Henry Purcell in the late seventeenth century. Elgar was a Catholic and his setting at the turn of the century of Cardinal Newman's poem about the journey of the soul after death, *The Dream of Gerontius*, proved highly controversial, though the oratorio eventually became part of the standard choral repertoire. Its musical vocabulary was Wagnerian and signalled England's musical rapprochement with the continent. Some of Elgar's music before the First World War expressed the confident imperial and national sentiment of the period. Slightly later composers like Vaughan Williams sought roots much further back among the Tudors, while Benjamin Britten turned to Purcell. One way and another, this was a recovery of the Great Tradition, further fertilised by the retrieval of folk music and the carol. This retrieval included a variety of cultural nationalism disliked by composers like Britten as the 'cow-pat' school of English composition.

We have the paradox of the agnostic Vaughan Williams writing popular hymns, editing the very influential collection *The English Hymnal* (1906), composing a mass and setting the great classic of English Puritan devotion *The Pilgrim's Progress*. Hubert Parry, Herbert Howells, Gustav Holst and William Walton were composers who sat loose to the Anglican tradition and yet contributed to the wealth of Anglican Church music. There was also an anti-Christian strain of vitalism represented by Delius' *Mass of Life* and, rather later, an Orthodox spirituality represented by John Tavener. At the same time there are the offerings of popular composers like Andrew Lloyd-Webber in *Joseph and his Amazing Technicolour Dream Coat* (1973) and *Jesus Christ Superstar* (1971).

So far I have referred to nationalism and political ideology in the context of the musical history of Britain and France. However, in the course of the nineteenth century nationalism suffused the whole of Europe as a principal vehicle of cultural identity and the retrieval of cultural memory, however distorted cultural identity and memory might often be. I intend to concentrate on nationalism and political ideology in Eastern Europe but it is worth briefly recollecting its influence throughout Europe. Spanish music provides an obvious case of composers like Da Falla, Turina, Granados and Albeniz, with a strong sense of the distinctive colours and dance rhythms of Spain. In Italy the operas of Verdi, for example, conveyed the composer's commitment to unification and the Risorgimento, and in Germany Wagner's operas expressed his commitment to the national ideal through the lens of myths in which humanity was its own redeemer through the charismatic powers of the individual creator. Scandinavian music was replete with rival forms of nationalism. Jean Sibelius above all expressed the landscape and spirit of Finland and looked back to its national myth the *Kalevala*. When the Danish composer Carl Nielsen set religious texts he may well have done so as an expression of the spirit of the folk. Edvard Grieg evoked the Norwegian scene without reference to established Lutheran Christianity, something you could certainly not say of Henrik Ibsen for whose *Pier Gynt* Grieg provided incidental music in 1875.

Nationalism in Eastern Europe is particularly interesting because it expressed the aspirations of peoples who gained their cultural, linguistic and political autonomy relatively late, especially as compared with countries like England and France that achieved territorial integrity centuries earlier. By the time of the revolutions of 1848, liberal nationalism and national autonomy were the overriding passions of the peoples of Eastern Europe. Antonin Dvořák was both a sincere Christian who wrote music for religious texts and a nationalist. Much of the music of the Hungarian Béla Bartók looks back to Hungarian folk tunes. Settings of biblical and liturgical texts often code national sentiment. For example, Leoš Janáček's *Glagolithic Mass* (1925) celebrates a folk occasion and witnesses to pan-Slavic aspirations and to ethnic roots in an ancient liturgical language. Zoltán Kodály's *Psalmus Hungaricus* (1923) sets the plight of post-war Hungary against the backdrop of the tribulations of ancient Israel.

Russia is one of the great musical powers and needs slightly more sustained attention because after 1917 it became the epicentre of an anti-religious political ideology more virulent even than the political ideologies of France and Turkey. Russian musical nationalism begins in the second quarter of the nineteenth century with an emphasis on folk styles and modal elements derived from Russian chant. Russian church music, like Russian music generally, experienced a tension between western and eastern influence, for example in the liturgical music of Dmitry Bortniansky, and Byzantine chant was eventually revived in a way which complemented the western plainsong revival centred on the monastery of Solesmes in France.

Glinka's patriotic opera *A Life for the Tsar* (1836) contained some oriental elements. The 'Russian five' (Balakirev, Cui, Borodin, Rimsky-Korsakov and Mussorgsky) were musical nationalists who used folk material. One also finds oriental elements in Balakirev's symphonic poem *Tamara*, Borodin's *Polovtzian Dances* and Rimsky-Korsakov's *Scheherazade*. Gradually throughout the nineteenth century folk styles were integrated into Russian composition. The first great Russian symphonist, Tchaikovsky, wrote mainly within a vibrant, visceral and sometimes melancholy Romantic style, with elements of programme music. Rachmaninoff developed a rich and sonorous late Romantic approach, especially in his three piano concertos, and his output included some important liturgical music, such as his Vespers. Prokofiev was another important composer who composed dissonant and difficult music in many genres and like Rachmaninoff immigrated after the Russian Revolution to the USA. However, he returned to Russia in the late 1930s and was eventually condemned for 'anti-democratic formalism'. The advent of the revolution in 1917 had resulted in the strict ideological regulation of music and Russia's most distinguished composer, Shostakovich, was obliged to accept 'just criticism'. His Leningrad symphony, finished in 1941, reflected soberly on the vast sufferings of the Russian people in the war.

We come now to my main contention concerning the return of the liturgical with the advent of modernism in music and in poetry. If we first take poetry in Britain, one of the most secular countries of the North Western European seaboard, the return of the liturgical is quite striking. Some of the main figures are T.S. Eliot, W.H. Auden and David Jones. More widely one might think of Rainer Maria Rilke and Paul Celan. It is difficult to exaggerate the influence of

Eliot or the shock he administered to the aesthetes of the Bloomsbury group when in the late 1920s he announced he had become a monarchist in politics and an Anglo-Catholic in religion. Musically it may be useful to indicate from almost random examples the kind of evidence that might underpin my argument. I am thinking of Poulenc and Messiaen in France, a composer like Hindemith setting Rilke's text *Marienleben*, Schönberg, Britten, Stravinsky, Schnittke, Gubaidulina, Penderecki, Górecki, Łukaszewski, Ešenvalds, Pärt, Tavener, Adams and James MacMillan. The compositions I have in mind are *Moses und Aron* which signalled Schönberg's return to Judaism, Bernstein's *Chichester Psalms* which was just one instance of the church's continuing role as patron, Barber's *Hermit Songs*, Copland's settings of Emily Dickinson, and operatic works where religious themes were central rather than incidental as in the *Ave Maria* in Verdi's *Otello*. Here the list is quite impressive, including Harrison's *The Last Supper*, John Adams' *El Niño* and *The Gospel according to the Other Mary* and Poulenc's *Dialogues des Carmélites* (1956). I suppose it would not be irrelevant here to cite composers like Will Todd, Jonathan Dove and John Rutter who have contributed to Anglican liturgical music.

We might take two major modern composers, Britten and Stravinsky, whose works indicate a major engagement with religious themes and texts. From Stravinsky we have the *Symphony of Psalms*, the *Requiem Canticles* and the *Mass*. From Britten we have a cornucopia of works with a religious frame or religious reference. He enriched the musical patrimony both of the Anglican and the Roman Catholic Church, for example the *Missa Brevis*. If one wanted to name two works that illustrate the ambiguous return of the sacred in modernism they might be Britten's *Sinfonia da Requiem* (1940) and the *War Requiem* set to the words of the First World War poet Wilfred Owen interspersed with the text of the liturgy, and first performed in the iconic site of the newly rebuilt Coventry Cathedral in 1962. Along with Britten and Stravinsky it would be worth paying particular attention to James MacMillan. Scotland 'should' have produced a post-Protestant nationalist composer. It got something very different: a devout Catholic whose music is centrally concerned with faith and liturgy. MacMillan is opposed to an anti-elitism that supposes an 'option for the poor' mandates an impoverished musical populism.

The examples I have given raise some interesting questions. Some of the composers cited come either from distinctly secular countries like England and Scotland, or from forcibly secularised countries like Russia, Estonia and Latvia. I find Arvo Pärt particularly interesting as a composer with a very wide appeal who comes from Estonia, arguably the most secular country in Europe. Schnittke is also interesting as a person of Jewish background who in Soviet times converted to Catholicism, while Sofia Gubaidulina came from a background of atheism and Tatar Islam to embrace a fervent Orthodox spirituality. The religious theme in Russian music under communism had its analogues in literature: Akhmatova, Mandelstam, Pasternak and Solzhenitsyn. By contrast, almost as though creative artists resist dominant trends, the USA may be a highly religious country but it has not produced composers with a feeling for liturgy, though Charles Ives does invoke something of the American Protestant religious and cultural background. It is not surprising that Polish composers under Russian occupation have written major religious works, for example Penderecki's *St. Luke Passion* (c.1965) and his *Polish Requiem* (c.1980), but it is worth noting the specific religious content compared (say) with the folk orientation of a major early twentieth-century composer, Karol Szymanowski. Maybe when confronted by a repressive atheist state you want to make it clear that you compose from the standpoint of explicit faith and not just cultural identity.

When we consider the revival of the liturgical there are some background factors worth remembering. There is a considerable audience for liturgical music sung by elite groups like Ex Cathedra and The Sixteen. That includes contemporary liturgical music sung by groups like Polyphony. Indeed the audiences for 'early' and modern liturgical music overlap and singers like Carolyn Sampson and Iestyn Davies are likely to perform polyphonic, baroque and modern music. So-called 'early music' extending from the Middle Ages to the Baroque and the early Enlightenment, and played with historical understanding on original instruments, owes a huge amount to pioneering groups like the Monteverdi Choir, founded in 1964, and the ability to explore lost repertoires afforded by contemporary technology, as well as associated changes in taste, such as the popularity of the counter-tenor voice.

But that only concerns background factors affecting taste over the last half century while the changes we are considering here go back eight or nine decades. They include the possibility of enjoying emotions of sublimity without the mundane inconveniences of long-term commitment. We may find some clues in the tortured search of T.S. Eliot as described in great detail by Robert Crawford in *The Young Eliot*, as well as changes in taste like the revival of Byzantine and Romanesque architecture.[7] Eliot began by exploring late nineteenth-century French poetry that was steeped in Catholicism to the point of using its language against it, in particular Laforgue and Baudelaire. Baudelaire pursued the fleeting pleasures of the moment in the 'modern' urban environment – he actually

---

[7]   Robert Crawford, *The Young Eliot: From St. Louis to the Waste Land*, London: Jonathan Cape, 2015.

invented the word 'modernity' assisted by drugs and the exploration of evil. Eliot belonged to the Bloomsbury group centred in London which deeply admired French culture and pursued a liberated and exploitative lifestyle. Eliot was profoundly damaged by the detritus of the last throes of Romanticism and sought a more objective and classical mode of living where the individual talent found itself in an organic relation to tradition.

In other words the depredations of Romantic individual 'genius' inverting all the values of respectability to create shock had run its course. Liturgy represented a collective form based on deep historical roots for which individual idiosyncrasy and the exploitation of personality was irrelevant. Moreover it reaffirmed the transcendent dimension in a fragmented world where 'nothing connects with nothing'. Eliot was concerned to centre the world in 'the temple', not to follow the path of those 'whose only monument was a thousand lost golf balls'. I have returned to my original argument about the distance between human brokenness in 'the world' including physical and spiritual death and the perspectives of 'the kingdom'. For Eliot, Christ was the good physician who plied the knife on the deep-seated infection.[8]

We have now to look further into the character of liturgy as a mirror of perfection and reconciliation in a ruined and fallen world. That is another way of saying that it codes both what Pascal called 'the misery of man' and what he called 'the grandeur of man'. It recognises just how far we have missed the mark *and* our aspiration to press, in the words of Paul, 'towards the mark of our high calling'. This is precisely what is meant by the rather abstract phrase 'an acute angle of transcendence'. However, an angle of transcendence, acute or otherwise, is not confined to what we conventionally label religion. It is a feature of the two most powerful rivals to religion: nationalism and utopian political ideology. Nationalism is a kind of collective transcendence that generates rituals, particularly to safeguard and express its demand for blood sacrifice from its male citizenry. Depending on particular historical circumstances it can co-operate with Christianity to create rituals that combine loyalty to the nation with Christian devotion, as in the USA or Britain, or it can attempt to suppress its public presence as in France or the Soviet Union.

However, both in France and Russia we have a union of nationalism with a universal utopian political ideology rather than with a universal religion. In the cases of France and Russia we encounter an acute angle of transcendence in political form. Political utopia holds that the gap between the way things are

---

[8]   T.S. Eliot. 'East Coker', section 4 of *The Four Quartets*, in *T.S. Eliot: Collected Poems*, p. 201.

and how they might be can be crossed and may be abolished given the right social conditions. It therefore wars against a specifically religious angle of transcendence because faith holds that the divine potential cannot be realised here on earth and remains 'above'. The persistence of religious rituals remains a sign of contradiction. In that sense utopian politics continue the sectarian tradition of Christianity which envisages the kingdom of God come on earth as it is in heaven, in particular through a refusal to countenance and participate in the institutions of human warfare. Here political utopianism mainly disagrees because, while one should not fight *solely* for the nation as a principle of division within humanity, one is bound to fight for the universal human good. Of course, in practice the nation is often defined in such a way that it is a first instalment of that universal good. America, for example, is defined as humanity's last and best hope, as was Russia in the 'great patriotic war'. We are once again back to attitudes to war as a basic diacritical marker.

That explains why, in what may look like an excursus, I want to take the rituals of the military as both cognate with religious rituals and defined over against them. I want to bring out the nature of Christian liturgy by exploring how it is simultaneously very like and very unlike military liturgies. After all, both Christian and military rituals are about death and the donation of blood and they concern brotherhood and camaraderie. At the same time a military chaplain is potentially an arena of acute moral tension. A central military principle is unquestioning obedience to command else the joint enterprise is imperilled. One cannot raise nice questions of moral propriety while under fire and the chaplain is a custodian of morale as much as a representative of morality. Military policy is determined to a very problematic extent by political necessity and the priority accorded success in battle.

This was precisely the point at issue with regard to the mass bombing of civilians in the Second World War. Secular thinking is very prone to suppose that mass bombing is wrong because it does not promote the victory it seeks to secure as soon as possible. This is a variety of sugared utilitarianism based on the assumption that what is morally wrong can never be politically right and the allied assumption that the world is so beneficently ordered that there is a happy coincidence between doing what is right and securing good and morally acceptable outcomes, at least in the long run. But there is no such happy coincidence. The mass bombing of civilians may not have been justifiable in terms of its efficacy in securing an end to hostilities, and the bombing of Dresden was totally unjustifiable,[9] but it is at least arguable that the use of the

---

9   Frederick Taylor, *Dresden: Tuesday 13 February 1945*, London: Bloomsbury, 2004.

atom bomb on Hiroshima in Japan saved many millions of lives, both allied *and* Japanese. The very severe Japanese military and civilian casualties on the island of Okinawa, which was the jumping off point for any potential invasion, is a relevant consideration here. Of course, if it were to be securely established that the Japanese were about to surrender *prior* to the dropping of the bomb, the argument for its use on Hiroshima would collapse. As for the bombing of Nagasaki, it at least seems clear that the Japanese had decided to surrender following the dropping of the Hiroshima bomb, so the dropping of the second bomb was unjustified.

In all these moral debates the facts of the matter are crucial for all participants who do not embrace an absolute prohibition on the use of violence. Calculations of the costs of alternatives in net suffering and loss of life are the constant coinage of debate about what should or should not have been done. One wants, indeed we all want, simultaneously to retain the benefits of a swift end to war in the Pacific and the right to be properly indignant about the appalling mass incineration of Japanese civilians. Some moral dilemmas are inherently tragic and can be solved neither by absolute principles nor cost-benefit analysis. Civilian war leaders make these decisions without consulting the citizen electorates, but were they to have done so in Britain, Australasia and America in the case of Japan, support for *any* means to end the horror of the Pacific war would have been overwhelming. Unfortunately, in such situations people all too easily think in terms of collective categories such as 'the Japanese' as well as in terms of collective guilt over time, even when that time extends over centuries.

At the same time as we engage in the proper exercise of conscientious reflection on tragic choices, there is also the priority accorded survival and success among those whose role is to execute policy in situations where even informed calculation is no more than a hunch as to likely consequences. The drive for survival and success includes the imperative of camaraderie and that in turn includes a demand for self-sacrifice on behalf of one's friends. It is at this point that the acute moral tension between the Christian imperative and the military imperative turns into something surprisingly like moral accord. 'Greater love hath no man than this, that he lay down his life for his friends.' 'They gave their today for our tomorrow.' The radical difference between the imperatives of Christianity and the imperatives of war is converted into a close analogy. Not only that, but the Christian vocabulary of spiritual warfare for the truth can easily be redeployed as a motive for the soldiers of Christ to enlist in physical warfare for humanity or the nation or civilisation or whatever. On a battle ship in the Pacific, American and British soldiers joined in singing 'Onward Christian soldiers/Marching as to war' easily eliding the difference between spiritual and physical warfare that the hymn itself acknowledges. Death in battle acquires mystical significance as in the case of what Geoffrey Hill called 'the mystery of the charity' of Charles Péguy, face down among the beetroots in northern France: '*Heureux ceux qui sont morts pour la terre charnelle*'.[10]

It may be that at this point it appears we have wandered from the theme of liturgy, but my argument is precisely that all these issues intersect. Liturgy is about the restoration of relationships that have been broken by violence. The problem of Christianity concerns the way in which concepts that had been spiritualised, like the concept of warfare, become materialised once again. The spiritual helmet of salvation becomes once more a material helmet, spiritual warfare becomes warfare plain and simple, and the cross is converted into a sword. Nothing could be more central to the argument of these commentaries than the way that under pressure from 'the world' and from our social nature (which is virtually the same thing) imagery becomes as malleable as principles are malleable. The detailed comparison between the liturgical action of arms and the Christian liturgy with its exchange of 'the peace', its benediction 'Peace be with you' and its concluding prayer for peace, *Dona nobis pacem*, is very much to the point.

The body language of the soldier differs from the body language of the priest as a march differs from a procession, and indicates a major difference of social function. The soldier advances in strict formation with automatic tread in order to dominate territory whereas the priest moves unemphatically forward at a civilian pace to minister to others in shared sacred space. Military gestures are designed to secure obedience whereas priestly gestures are designed to include in the embrace of peace or to consecrate or to bless. Military dress hugs the outline of the body to facilitate the maximum and immediate mobilisation of physical force, whereas priestly dress flows and envelops. Nevertheless both vestments and uniforms mark secure hierarchy and indicate the locus of authority. In neither case can there be jostling for place since hierarchy has been established from the outset. The difference in body language between army and church is matched by the difference between church music and military music. Marching music explores a very limited space of transcendence between quick and energising and slow and elegiac, because the army is concerned with such limited social order as may be possible. Church music by contrast explores the whole range of transcendence between human limitation and divine and human potential and possibility.

---

[10]   Charles Sisson, quoting Péguy, in 'Charles Péguy', in Charlie Louth and Patrick McGuinness (eds) *A C.H. Sisson Reader*, Manchester: Carcanet/Fyfield, 2014, p. 185.

But the army and the church do come together at two powerful emotional junctions. One is the slow concerted movement of people with banners. The Song of Songs has the extraordinary phrase 'terrible as an army with banners, and his banner over me was love'. The processional movement of the cross is the advance of the banners of love: 'The royal banners forward go' – *Vexilla Regis prodeunt*. The other moment of powerful conjunction concerns the commemoration of sacrifice. The church and the army both commemorate sacrifice and the gift of blood.

Now that we have explored the similarity and the difference between two major modes of representing social order, we need to turn to the nature of liturgy itself. In the first place it is antithetical to Romantic notions of the exploitation of ego and personality. The return of liturgy is precisely the return of the collective and the impersonal, and of the universal rather than the personalised particular. It is not the result of romantic grand gestures but the net consequence of minute and co-ordinated accretions: people engaged in small discrete actions that build up an ensemble. It works like an orchestra or a theatre company in that it depends on the spirit of the whole to co-ordinate individual actions. It is in fact a small miracle of detailed co-operation between people who know exactly how and when they should perform their delimited roles. These add up to a complex choreography that could, in principle, be reduced to a form of notation. For example, the notation deals with entrances and exits, speech and silence, the handling of material elements, individual and collective utterance, the phasing of liturgical mode from petition and obeisance to celebration and anamnesis. Perhaps it is worth remembering here the military term, 'detail', which refers to the way people are detailed to deal with particular spheres of action.

Let us now look more closely at the phases through which the action of liturgy must pass, because liturgy takes a particular and determinate shape. It leads the participants through a known and familiar sequence with understood variants. In particular it orders time in a familiar cycle following the natural seasons and co-ordinates them with a narrative sequence that moves forwards to a known crisis and redemptive resolution. It also reaches a point of fulfilment in the recognition of presence and theophany: *Agios o theos, agios isichiros, agios athanatos imas*. It recognises the depredations of division through confession and seeks resolution through the restoration of communion. The participant begins with acknowledgement of separation, and then through gestures of inclusion and blessing experiences reconciliation and peace. Gestures of peace and inclusion govern the whole of liturgical action. The distance between a moral ruin and transcendence is closed by the operation of grace.

Given what liturgy seeks to achieve in terms of recognition of ruin and restoration of relationships through grace, it is not difficult to see why, with the advent of modernity in the arts and music, the experience of dislocation and fragmentation has been responded to by a return to liturgy.

On Peaceable Wisdom as Mediating between Radical Eschatology and Brute Reality

I have suggested that in primitive Christianity there is, as in Buddhism, an acute angle of transcendence compared with other examples of the Axial revolution, especially Islam. In Islam God is certainly transcendent in his power and compassion but the political ethics of Islam accept the stark realities of our personal and political existence with a minimum of tension. The protest in principle against these realities embodied in pacifism or monasticism is virtually absent except maybe on the margins of Sufism.

I have also suggested that in the course of Christian history an acute angle of transcendence generates a dichotomy between the ideal kingdom hovering above history and the ordinary quotidian world where life is regulated by the exercise of preponderant power resting ultimately on sedimented but at the same time firmly legitimated violence. The ideal kingdom acts upon the world as a template embodying a radical difference between the ideal and everyday realities. It is the kingdom of what is 'not yet' and remains beyond realisation as a political possibility. At the same time there are pressures to bring it about on earth as in heaven. A time is envisaged, for example in the Book of Revelation 11:15, when 'the kingdoms of this world shall become the kingdom of our God and of his Christ, and he shall reign for ever and ever'. The Christian creed seems to entertain a firm anticipation of a time when Christ will come into a kingdom that has no end. Christ, according to the first epistle to the Corinthians 15:28, will hand those who are his over to the Father, and God will be 'all in all'. This corresponds to the hope of the psalmist, for whom one day the earth will be full of the glory of God.

I summarise yet again this eschatological expectation in order to introduce a third possibility between the realities of violence and the establishment of a divine kingdom of universal peace where nation no longer rises up against nation and history as we know it comes to an end. There have, of course, been many versions of this eschatological end to history from Marx's projected age of communism to Francis Fukuyama's expected triumph of liberalism, and modern theological visions of demythologisation and the emptying of God into history from Rudolph Bultmann to Harvey Cox.

The third possibility is a version of the Age of the Holy Spirit as set out by Joachim of Fiore but shorn of triumphal expectations and directly material manifestations of divine government here on earth. Its primary source in Scripture is the Wisdom tradition in the later books of the Hebrew Scriptures and it softens the angle of transcendence in the eschatological anticipations of both Old Testament and New Testament. It might even be called the Third Way of the Third Person. The book of Proverbs 4:6 declares that we should 'love wisdom and she will safeguard you'. So the path of wisdom has a feminine face. Wisdom is demonstrated in quality of life rather than logical demonstration. The wise man is not the clever man but someone whose way of life exemplifies wholeness and integrity and whom you trust for disinterested counsel. A Christmas prayer speaks of Wisdom leaping down from the seat of the Most High but coming to dwell among us: a divine presence of mind taking up residence in the house of the intellect to temper and inform it. Obviously this is an idealisation but it is at the same time an ideal to be held up as a mode of human governance. Wisdom or *Sapientia* is not so much knowledge about this or that as she is an animating spirit which in the words of Scripture 'plays all over the earth' and lies at the heart of Genesis and Creation. She is participatory. She also offers the contentment and satisfaction of being absorbed in practical activity or contemplation without the pressure of some overriding objective or subjection to the endlessly rotating gyroscope of desire. She encourages a 'wise passiveness'.[1]

If we turn from the contemplation of wisdom to the issues of human and humane governance we have to think about what Jerusalem as a city has meant in human history. There are two trajectories. One follows the line of a spiritual Jerusalem seen as the 'mother of us all' and the universal inheritance of a redeemed humanity. The ideal city takes many embodiments. One is the sacred ecology of the spaces in Paris that historically included Notre Dame and *La Sainte Chapelle*. Another is a Christian city like Venice or Rome. Venice saw itself ideally as the enlightened city, the gate of heaven and herald of redemption.

The actual history of Venice in dealing with rivals like Aquilea was otherwise, and we are dealing with a mythic and self-serving projection. But humanity often envisages the perfect and realises it in imperfection, recognising that the perfect is often the enemy of the good. The heavenly city, imagined as a part

---

[1]   William Wordsworth, 'Expostulation and Reply', in William Wordsworth, *Selected Poems*, London: Penguin, 1996, p. 200.

of a Christian Enlightenment, was a mythic projection of brotherly love like all political dreams, but it found some partial realisation in Philadelphia. Even the monastery as generated by a more acute angle of transcendence could be visualised as the heavenly city come on earth. The Abbey church of Melk, high above the Danube, was the theatre of God's glory where sacred and secular power came together. At its heart it had a fresco depicting the New Jerusalem and looked onto a paradise garden with streams of living water and abundant fruits to gladden the heart of man. The world's major faiths each in their own way imagine a mild angle of transcendence with paradise gardens and holy cities. Gardens and cities go together.

In 2004 the historian Tristram Hunt published a book about New Jerusalem built here among what the visionary William Blake called 'these dark satanic mills'.[2] He traced the origins of urban planning in the deadly murk and literal pandemonium of the Industrial Revolution: Joseph Chamberlain and the Municipal Gospel in Birmingham, visions of civic spaces and city parks in Leeds, Glasgow and New York, the new creation of places like Letchworth, Welwyn Garden City and Bourneville that half-realised the dreams of the Quaker Ebenezer Howard in his *Garden Cities of Tomorrow*. Most of these ventures of the imagination were interim realisations of hope and faith where the kingdom of God was not a template for the ideal city or even a story of return from Babylonian exile to rebuild Jerusalem against the assaults of her enemies. They are what Francis Thompson in his poem 'The Kingdom of God' (subtitled 'In no Strange Land') called the world invisible that we view and the world intangible that we touch, a place where love takes precedence over what Wordsworth denounced as 'getting and spending'.[3] Some imagined places of fraternity and community end up far from their point of origin. Saltaire retains something of the vision of Titus Salt even though it is suspended in time by conservation, and Canterbury in New York State is much as the Shakers imagined it. But Bethlehem, Pennsylvania, as a steel town dedicated among other things to weaponry, evolved a long way from the original Moravian settlement. Le Corbusier's messianic dreams entered the mainstream to become normal and banal. The renovation of Bermondsey in London by Christian doctors and politicians like Alfred Salter ended up a developer's dream town.

All this is poetry and imagination, but it is poetry and imagination consonant with major strains in both Old and New Testaments. I have already suggested

---

[2]   Tristram Hunt, *Building Jerusalem: The Rise and Fall of the Victorian City*, London: Weidenfeld and Nicolson, 2004.

[3]   William Wordsworth, 'The World and Our Spirits', in Wordsworth, *Selected Poems*, p. 153.

that the Eucharist is the similitude of the perfect society, rooted and grounded in the giving and receiving of the Saviour's life blood. W.H. Auden returns us to the reality of the Christian city as a site of atonement. In the 'Vespers' poem from the sequence 'Horae Canonicae' he contrasts two opposed types, the idealist and the realist, and contrives their meeting at a crossroads.[4] The meeting forces both to confront the unpalatable half of the truth which the other represents. The idealist must accept the shedding of blood and the realist the innocence of their joint victim:

> For without cement of blood (it must be human, it must be innocent) no secular wall will safely stand.

---

[4]   W.H. Auden, 'Horae Canonicae', in *W.H. Auden: Collected Poems* (ed. Edward Mendelson), London: Faber & Faber, 1976, p. 484.

Afterword

'The impact of the Bible on Christian conceptions of history, from the earliest Christian centuries to the nineteenth, was radical and pervasive.'[1] John Burrow, in *A History of Histories*, traces the profound consequences of the model provided in the Hebrew Scriptures of a chosen people who are subjected by God to 'a recurrent pattern of transgression, punishment and deliverance'. This pattern is transferred to Christendom within an overall framework of Adam's sin, Christ's salvation and the expectation of final judgement as the end of history. This same pattern is also transferred to sects and to nations, so that we have a virtually endless replication of the idea of being chosen as God's elect. Nineteenth-century nationalism was an ideology that picked up the earlier donations of theology as set forth in biblical history, with momentous consequences.

John Burrow presents a particularly lucid version of some of my fundamental arguments about the way 'Chosenness' breeds progeny in terms of peoples and nations claiming divine or historical election. But I also need to enquire more closely into the fount and origin of this prolific idea in Judaism and its sacred book the Bible, and for that I turn to the treatment of the Bible provided by a Jewish author, Eric Auerbach, in his classic study *Mimesis*.[2] Auerbach provides us with an overall summary of his approach to the representation of reality in European literature, based on a contrast between Homeric writing and Old Testament writing. I use Eric Auerbach to complement John Burrow through his analysis of the fundamental modes and implications of biblical writing, using Homer's writing at very roughly the same period to bring out these implications by way of dramatic contrast.

Auerbach provides a generalised contrast between two basic kinds of writing that permeate all European literature and the writing of history. The Homeric epic is a fully 'externalised' description with all events carefully delineated in the foreground, nothing unstated or mysterious, without development of character

---

[1]   John Burrow, *A History of Histories: Epics, Chronicles, Romances and Inquiries from Herodotus and Thucydides to the Twentieth Century*, London: Penguin, 2007, p. 182.

[2]   Eric Auerbach, *Mimesis: The Representation of Reality in Western Literature*, trans. Willard R. Trask, Princeton, NJ: Princeton University Press, 1953.

or contradictory layers of meaning and demanding no more than enchanted engagement with the tale. The biblical style demands a quite different kind of engagement: it presents some aspects in high relief and leaves others in obscurity, it contains a multiplicity of meanings and a preoccupation with the problematic, and, crucially, it makes 'universal historical claims'. Auerbach makes incisive comments that pertain very directly to the issues discussed in this book, notably the hand of providence and of God in history. He writes of the biblical narrative: 'The sublime influence of God here reaches so deeply into the everyday that the two realms of the sublime and the everyday are not only actually unseparated but basically inseparable.'[3] The rest of Auerbach's comments mostly follow directly from this primary involvement of God in the narrative action. He claims that the writing of 'the Eloist' in the Old Testament is an assertion of 'absolute authority' requiring belief. The nub is that

> all other scenes, issues and ordinances ... the history of all mankind, will be given their due place within its frame, will be subordinated to it. The scripture stories do not, like Homer's, court our favor, they do not flatter us that they may please and enchant us – they seek to subject us, and if we refuse to be subjected we are rebels.[4]

I am not in any way an enlightened rebel, since I find a constant source of sustenance in the narrative of the Hebrew Scriptures. Moreover, I am not opposed to the idea of the presence of God but to his supposed activity as a power that shapes history from above and micro-manages it for the sake of a particular elect people. The issue is election and micro-management. I do not doubt the presence of God, for example, in various epiphanies and theophanies. But as regards this key point, relating to the whole of human history turning on a detailed providential plan of God with the chosen people at the centre, it seems to me unsustainable.

In this book I have argued that the religions of the Axial Age, above all Christianity and Buddhism, represent absolute presuppositions, not in the

---

3   Auerbach, *Mimesis*, pp. 22–3.

4   Auerbach, *Mimesis*, p. 15. Auerbach also makes penetrating comments on the New Testament, above all the scene of Peter's betrayal, which he describes as a unique and direct conversation between an unlettered fisherman and a serving-maid such as could not, and does not, occur anywhere in classical literature. 'What we witness is the awakening of "a new heart and a new spirit"' (p. 43). Auerbach also writes about the profound impact of Jesus on people he encounters: 'The random fisherman or publican or rich youth, the random Samaritan or adulteress, come from their random everyday circumstances to be immediately confronted with the personality of Jesus: and the reaction of an individual in such a moment is necessarily a matter of profound seriousness, and very often tragic' (p. 44).

philosophical sense but in terms of attitudes to 'the world', in radical opposition to the dynamics of human violence. Restricting myself to Christianity, I suggest that its opposition to 'the world' generates a coherent grammar that passes through characteristic transformations in response to the realities of violence. These are embedded in a providential Jewish history, the moral implications of which, with respect to the character of God, cannot be sustained. Christianity develops the providential history of the Jews as a divine plan with identical unsustainable moral implications for the character of God. Certain versions of the doctrine of atonement, understood as part of a divine plan, are morally unsustainable in a particularly obvious way. In other words, the Christian appropriation of the Jewish providential reading of history has to be jettisoned on moral grounds rather than empirical or 'evidential' ones. Evidential grounds are entirely secondary given that you can, with considerable effort, read history as 'evidence' for God's providential care for his people, whether construed as the Jews or as the New Israels of Christianity. There is clearly an alternative reading of sacred history, which I do not intend to follow through, that might focus on the despair of the Jewish Israel and the Christian and nationalist New Israels at God's indifference to their fate. I mean that the Bible could be read more as documenting despair at divine indifference than as an expression of faith and hope in his promises. This indifference breeds a paradoxical attempt to force the hand of history through exemplary violence, which acts as a *Doppelgänger* of the more pervasive accommodation with things as they are until God interrupts history with a Final Judgement that ushers in his reign of perpetual peace. This supposition has innumerable secular translations in terms of political myths of progress towards the instauration of peace and justice.

This is where we return to the absolute presuppositions of Christianity and their subsequent grammar. This grammar is manifested in the New Testament narratives of the priorities of 'the kingdom' over against 'the world', and the narrative of the Passion as the direct and inevitable consequence of those priorities. There is no way in which one can separate an understanding of 'the kingdom' from its consequences in the narrative of the Passion. If one has jettisoned the Jewish and Christian understanding of the working out of a divine plan, one is driven to articulate a naturalistic understanding of the Christian narratives of Incarnation, Kingdom and Passion as present in the structure of experience, given the opposition of Christianity and 'world'. This book seeks to provide that naturalistic understanding. It also hopes to show how the Christian liturgy seeks to reconcile, within a concentrated drama, the regime of violence, culminating in the condemnation and humiliation of the innocent, written in the body of the Saviour, with the symbolic achievement of peace and restoration. This book assumes that the drama of the liturgy as enacted in Baptism and Eucharist summarises in the most concentrated symbolic form possible the movement from violence to reconciliation. The liturgy encompasses my book's title: ruin and restoration. Of course, the regime of violence in the world is not abrogated by either its Christian or its secular oppositions, but the liturgical enactment of reconciliation stands as an ever renewed alternative vision and anamnesis. These realisations cannot be occluded by the iteration of pious phrases that, even if they do not directly endorse the providential reading of history, avoid confronting the inevitable alternative.

In the more extended discussion that follows I do not develop further the working out of the transformational grammar of Christianity in the course of Christian history. That has been the burden of almost all my sociological work. Rather, I tease out what it is to engage with Christian faith and with the Bible if one has dispensed with the idea of a providential ordering of history where God pulls the strings behind the stage, in particular as that is worked out in a doctrine of atonement through penal substitution. I conclude by trying to bring together what I believe to be the thematic repertoire of the Gospels, without repeating the discussions in the commentaries. Let me now bring together my conclusions in this book as succinctly as I can before I turn to how, as a priest of the Anglican Church I understand the Gospels.

I think that Christianity as originally preached and practised embodies an acute angle of transcendence that allies it to Buddhism more than any other orientation of the 'Axial Age' either side of the divide between bc and ad, especially with regard to violence. Violence, in which I include violation, is the fulcrum of my analytic focus, and primitive Christianity in its proclamation of the kingdom and its narrative of the Passion embraces a profound rejection of violence. That is the case even though I notice an oscillation in the Scriptural narratives and in Christian history between eschatological withdrawal and attempts violently to bring in the kingdom. Both responses derive from the same acute angle of transcendence.

As a consequence of his profound rejection of violence Jesus suffers a radical violation of his physical body and the break-up of the body of his followers through treachery and denial. This consequence need not be regarded as an interpretive theological move but can be understood as the likely social consequence of non-violence. This is simply what happens. This is what non-violence entails and it is very costly. Christianity codes the cost in the cross and re-presents a realism that is starkly outlined for all to see, supposing they have eyes to see. Mostly we prefer an evasive gloss because none of us can bear very much reality. There is no lesion such as Bernard Shaw in his play *Major Barbara* proposed between the primitive Christian construal of the violent dynamic of 'the world', and what he denigrated as Crosstianity. The one entails the other as a consequence that may be anticipated on the basis of social observation *alone*.

As an adolescent, painfully emerging from the revivalist Evangelicalism of my father, a chauffeur and taxi-driver who left school at 11, I was much influenced by Shaw's combination of adamant pacifism, related to Tolstoy's understanding of the kingdom of God as preached on the Sermon on the Mount, and his political translation of Christianity into a characteristically British socialism. After a period of atheism, Shaw embraced an early version of Process Theology linked to Bergsonian creative evolution. What I picked up from Shaw was a profoundly individualistic Protestantism that rejected all Christian institutional forms and dissolved them in a variety of personal mysticism. This mysticism was characterised by Troeltsch as a major modern form of spiritual Christianity. In particular, Shavian mysticism attacked the doctrine of atonement as a way of shuffling off personal responsibility, and it attacked aspects of the Abrahamic and Mosaic God as imperious, punitive and morally objectionable. It asked what kind of God could render a man childless for marrying his brother's widow: notoriously this was the text at the heart of Henry VIII's divorce from Catherine of Aragon.

Coming from thinkers like Shaw, or for that matter from Richard Dawkins, this criticism of aspects of the God of the Hebrew Scriptures is accepted as legitimate, whereas coming from a Christian it is treated as illegitimate on account of the appalling history of Christian anti-Semitism. Interestingly, Rabbi Jonathan Sachs (in a BBC debate 16/9/2012) accused Richard Dawkins of being influenced by Christian anti-Semitism, to Dawkins' considerable discomfort. However, the issue is not whether criticism of aspects of the Abrahamic God is influenced by anti-Semitism but whether the objections are morally sustainable. In my view they are, and they are consistent with the central implications of Christianity. They lie at the heart of the radical revision of Judaism found in the New Testament, which is precisely what I have argued in this book. I have also argued that the providential view of history set forth in the Hebrew Scriptures is a precursor of the various teleological understandings of history found in numerous secular and utopian ideologies, notably nationalism and communism. As I have already indicated, John Burrow summarises this comprehensively and eloquently.

Here I need to refer to two other crucial influences on my thinking. One is Karl Popper on *The Poverty of Historicism* (1957) which released me from all varieties of teleological history, and the other is Reinhold Niebuhr whose *Moral Man and Immoral Society* (1932) released me from the utopian illusions of pacifism and converted me to a realist view of the operations of human society put forward throughout this book. I describe this process in my intellectual autobiography, *The Education of David Martin*.[5] The writings of Reinhold Niebuhr, for example in his work on Christian ethics and his *The Nature and Destiny of Man* (1941), and for that matter, of Richard Niebuhr in his work on *Christ and Culture* (1951), reintroduced me to the riches of an institutional and liturgical Christianity as understood within an Augustinian perspective. This reintroduction was reinforced, in adolescence and my early twenties, by an extensive reading of Anglican apologists such as Quick, Gore, Farrer and Temple and Catholic apologists beginning with Chesterton and Martin D'Arcy. I realised that the individualistic translation of Christianity in the form of a debased Protestantism lacked any sense of the profundity found in collective versions of Christian faith. This was further reinforced and deepened by my eventual understanding of the social sciences as a critique of atomistic individualism and its delusions.

Contemporary secular pacific sentiment exhibits the ethical stance but refuses to face the cost it entails. Insofar as the cross makes some contemporary sense, it is assimilated to a version of secular idealism and Jesus is treated as someone who paid for his ideals in a particularly horrible but admirable way. The costly entailment signified and re-presented by the cross is unacceptable to the point where righteous sentiments can be publicly paraded without the realistic choices and costs ever being faced. You stand back with arms folded in horror at the costs of choice, perpetually reserving your position in order not to pay the price of concrete choices as well as to retain in perpetuity the irresponsible pleasures of righteousness. And you bolster your position through the deployment of coercive comparisons with whatever past situation best suits your present book. If you want to intervene in some imbroglio you cite a historical sequence where the net consequences of intervention can plausibly be regarded as avoiding worse outcomes. And vice versa.

---

[5]   David Martin, *The Education of David Martin: The Making of an Unlikely Sociologist*, London: SPCK, 2014. Popper's views, read on a train to Newport in 1958 in the course of reading an External London degree in Sociology by correspondence course, released me in something like a conversion experience from a combination of teleological Marxism and liberalism, and combined with my reading of Herbert Butterfield's critique of such ideas in his *The Whig Interpretation of History* (1931) laid the groundwork for my other major pre-occupation: secularisation understood as written into the historical process. Popper and Butterfield together made possible my exposure, in 1965, of the combination of teleological and empirical elements in secularisation theory, and my attempt, in 1969, to combine a theory of general empirical tendencies towards secularisation with major historical inflections.

The original Christian angle of transcendence is clean contrary to the observed dynamic of what in the Gospels Christianity calls 'the world'. Like all radical visions it has to be bent back to accommodate that dynamic on account of its long historical experience of the often quite limited possibilities that realistically exist. Here it differs from its closest relative, Judaism, and from its much more distant relative Islam. In fact Judaism and Islam are not confronted with, nor are they affronted by, the violent dynamic of 'the world' to anything like the same degree, and they are therefore less exercised by the need for accommodation. Neither sex nor violence and the violence associated with sexuality are as radically problematic as they are in Christianity and the cultures it has influenced. The same applies to the dynamic of economic accumulation and to the inherent dubieties of political action and of political inaction, given that inaction can be as consequential as action.[6] An accommodated Christianity has to go through major and often quite rapid adjustments to achieve its rapprochement with 'the world' to the point where it becomes simultaneously a very effective vehicle of 'the world' and its profane dynamic, while at the same time subverting it. Adam Seligman, as a Jew, regards Christianity as the most radical and important revolution in history and laments his Harvard students' ignorance of it in their exclusive devotion to technique, but he believes that Christian radicalism has put everything at hazard and dangerously 'upped the ante', especially in its relative neglect of ritual and its relentless pursuit of sincerity. Christianity represents a wager that might not come off and it is impossible not to sympathise with his critique of sincerity and defence of ritual rectitude.[7]

As Adam Seligman also emphasises, Christianity owes virtually everything to Judaism, its tropes, its exemplary stories, its images and its motifs. Even Christianity's universalism is initially inflected by its Jewish origins and the special covenant God has with the Jewish people. Paul, in his Epistle to the Ephesians 2:11-22, provides a magnificent summary of Christian universalism, but it is still influenced by Jewish historical privilege. He argues that the Gentiles, once outside and alien, 'having no hope and without God in the world', have now been included as part of the commonwealth of Israel 'by the blood of Christ'. These passages in Ephesians about those who were once distant being brought close, about Christ, our peace, having broken down every partition, about the creation of access to the Father through the one Spirit and about the end of

---

[6] This is another of those cases where Reinhold Niebuhr's contrast between the moralisation possible at the political level compared with what is possible at the interpersonal level is too sharp.

[7] Adam Seligman, *Modernity's Wager: Authority, the Self and Transcendence*, Princeton, NJ: Princeton University Press, 2003.

enmity realised in the all-inclusive body provide one of the supreme statements of universalism.

Yet Jesus, as Christianity's founder, lived and worked within Jewish presuppositions, whatever radical revisions he embraced in terms of devotion to internal sincerity rather than external conformity, in particular ritual rectitude, or in the recognition he accorded people outside Israel, like the Samaritan woman at the well. The contrast of inward and outward, together with a suspicion of the efficacy of ritual rectitude, is today part of what Christianity has donated to culture, but its origins clearly lie within Judaism. The immersion of Christianity in the particular culture of Judaism, and in the way it frames its characteristic dilemmas, is what the conception in Paul's epistle to the Philippians chapter 2 about self-emptying and 'taking the form of a servant' entails. A saviour outside culture and equipped with a universal answer book would be inhuman and monstrous. The knowledge and experience of the saviour was limited by context and we cannot straightforwardly extrapolate from sayings and pronouncements made in that milieu to our contemporary context. We saturate ourselves in those pronouncements through close and responsible reading but we cannot straightforwardly read off contemporary answers.

In any case, these pronouncements are in a literary genre responding, often hyperbolically, to particular situations, and we notoriously select from them for our own rhetorical purposes. They are in a profound way 'indignant' reactions where indignation reflects what is not 'dignus', not worthy. The Gospels are about what is worthy and unworthy. Proof texting to achieve a predetermined and triumphant conclusion about this or that moral issue is an unworthy game. To say that the saviour made such and such a pronouncement is to open a discussion within a shared hermeneutic tradition not to foreclose it. In any case, different situations drew forth contradictory responses, supposing we had confidence that these were indeed the words of Jesus. We are, after all, contemporary moral agents gifted by virtue of our humanity with responsibility.

Nevertheless, when all is said and accepted about the saturation of Christianity in the Hebrew Scriptures, and about 'Jesus the Jew' as in the main speaking prophetically to other Jews, what emerges from the Judaic matrix is very different from it.[8] That difference is often attributed to Greek influences, and these are certainly important when it comes to the Wisdom tradition. No matter that the New Testament narrative is informed throughout by typological understandings derived from the Hebrew Scriptures, what transpires on the basis of an acute angle of transcendence with respect to violence, sex and

---

[8]   Geza Vermes, *Jesus the Jew*, London: SCM, 2011.

economic 'goods' is astonishingly different. It is so different that I have gone so far as to suggest that the notion of the Abrahamic religions is a useful political fiction emanating in particular from the presuppositions of American political culture. To worship one God is not to worship the same God. The blank space of the incomprehensible God of 'Judaism' (the concept of Judaism being itself a dubious if defensible coinage) in covenant with a particular and 'peculiar' people is utterly unlike the God whose 'express image' is found in an humiliated human body and in a disfigured human face where 'sorrow and love flow mingled down' for us and for our salvation. Golgotha is the place where Christians see placarded the cost of salvation and also receive assurance that they are covered and justified by the action of redeeming love.

Sophisticated commentators may talk about 'Being Itself' high above all existents, but Christianity's claim is precisely that being's self has come to be in human existence. To Judaism and Islam alike, this is an intolerable blasphemy and has been so since it was condemned as such by the high priest in the Passion narrative. In his notion of 'the olive tree' in his epistle to the Romans chapter 11, Paul tried to retain God's particular covenant with Judaism and its cultural presuppositions, while stretching out on something like a logical rack towards universalism. He tried to retain God's special relationship with the Jews while simultaneously superseding it. It could not be done and it cannot be done. The Christian Eucharist may be modelled on the Jewish Passover, just as the lectionaries for Holy Week clearly suggest. Nevertheless Eucharist and Passover are very different, even though I have participated with gratitude in a Jewish Passover in Jerusalem.[9]

What Jonathan Sacks calls 'the dignity of difference' needs to be respected and not abandoned in some airy supposition that underneath all religions, or at any rate those we opportunistically choose to count as respectable, say the same thing because relating to the same God. They do not, and their Gods are not versions of each other, however much as faiths they may also have in common or however much they may contain shadow images of each other.

Here I come once again to the special care exercised by the Jewish God for his special people. I need to be very clear: I am in no way setting aside the central Hebraic contribution to our moral sensibility or turning away from all that can be gained from a close reading of, and a committed engagement with, the Hebrew Scriptures: on the contrary. After all I do precisely that nearly every Sunday, and Christian priests and ministers repeat the psalms every month. The psalms in particular are their meat and drink. The Hebrew Scriptures provide us

---

[9] A Portuguese *seder* with the family of Professor Zvi Werblowski.

with our exemplary stories and our cast of characters as opposed to our abstract reasoning. They illustrate our vocabulary of motives and provide our thematic repertoire. Take for example the theme of ultimate sacrifice and reprieve in the story of Abraham and Isaac, or the theme of making hostile judgements and somehow excepting oneself from those judgements as found in the story of the prophet Nathan's confrontation with King David. The Hebrew Scriptures speak of breathing life into dry bones and dead bodies; of the rigours of journeying in the wilderness and the wilderness blossoming as the rose; of choosing life not death; of torrents of judgement on the oppressors of the poor; of hospitality to the stranger; of wisdom, virtue and vanity; of law and statute as guides to righteous living and the centrality of doing justly, loving mercy and walking humbly; of the love that many waters cannot quench; of exile and home coming; of the desecrated city and hope of deliverance; of dreams and visions; of the misery and littleness of man and his grandeur; of still waters, the valley of the shadow and a table set for a feast; of the God who reveals his majesty and the God who hides himself and evades all characterisation or is overheard in the still, small voice.

What does not make sense to me is the idea that God exercises a particular care for a particular people, either in its Jewish or its Christian or its Islamic form or its endless nationalistic derivatives characterised in the quotation above from John Burrow. That God whirls other peoples around in various assorted mayhems for the moral benefit of particular peoples has to be a narcissistic delusion. The idea of Providence is morally unsustainable at any and every level, personal or historical. Jonathan Sacks may believe that the Exodus story shows God's concern for the oppressed but that is an astonishingly dubious claim given the historical record. The Exodus story is indeed a story of liberation that has assisted Israel's struggle to survive. It has inspired many oppressed peoples and in Christian terms it provides a powerful typological metaphor of triumph over sin and death. But it is also shot through with morally objectionable suppositions culminating in the all too alluring idea of a promised land and the dispensability of other peoples. The story asks us to believe in divine actions directed against whole peoples by way of collective punishment, such as the elimination by divine decree of all the first-born of the Egyptians and the ethnic cleansing of peoples in the supposedly promised land. Yes, there is also much about care for the stranger within the gates, but there is no getting around the immoral implications of a providence working for Jewish or any other interests, including moral interests. God's ways are certainly past finding out and not 'as our ways', but they cannot be mysterious along that particular model. We are all equally subject to universal contingency in a way that brings us to ask just why we have been abandoned.

Only the mistaken idea of providence could generate that most terrible and most human of cries from the cross and thereby place God exactly in our situation to redeem us and it: 'My God, my God, why hast thou forsaken me?'

I come to this conclusion intellectually, but I am simultaneously driven to it on the basis of pastoral experience. This is another instance of the experiential being also the empirical on account of the inbuilt causal sequences of any moral vision that seeks consistency. My pastoral experience is constantly repeated in the experience of Christian priests and ministers. One parishioner rich in years rejoiced in the power of prayer (allied to the skill of physicians) to give a reprieve from the threat of a lethal cancer. Another simply lamented the sudden loss of her middle-aged son to deadly disease and saw no reason to suppose that prayer might have altered the outcome in his favour or to suppose that other than natural processes are in play. God had nothing whatever to do with it. A third parishioner lamented the loss of her son in his mid-twenties and could not make sense of it except to believe that God wanted her 'lovely son' for himself. This is a pagan idea but recast in Christian terms. There was a higher purpose at work. The first and the third responses assume the action of providence.

But this idea of a plan and micro-management in relation to prayer is not necessarily confined to relatively unreflective people. It can be found in the theologians I most admire. In an admirable short book by Rowan Williams, *Being Christian*, in the section on prayer, the author glosses the advice of Origen in the third century. If God already knows what we want and what we are going to do, and he obviously does, why pray? 'God has decided to work out his purposes *through* what we decide to say and do', 'so', adds Williams 'you'd better get on with it'.[10] This assumes some compatibility between our desires and the overall moral governance of God as well as the possibility of harmonising our various requests and, presumably, excludes requests for favoured treatment. That in turn would mean that no particular request was dealt with favourably because it would have to be set against competing requests to bring them into alignment. It sounds rather like C.S. Lewis' claim that God takes our wishes into account in managing all the infinite number of variables he has to organise in bringing about his purposes for the world. This seems to me to impinge on human freedom and to imply micro-management on an unimaginable scale by a God who was a moral super-computer. I should not like to live in such a world.

This seems to me pretty dubious at the personal level and intolerable at the historical and collective level. It loads the responsibility for history on to God.

---

10   Rowan Williams, *Being Christian: Baptism, Bible, Eucharist, Prayer*, London: SPCK, 2014, p. 65.

There is no providential guiding hand that can be jogged by prayer to foster a particular person, interest, people or cause. We use pious phrases as covering notes for this obvious absence of providence, as for example, when we ask God or thank God for 'a happy issue out of all our afflictions'. Once we try and cash these phrases their lack of fiduciary backing is obvious, should we allow ourselves to think about it, which we mostly do not. Paper money without backing will serve to cover the gaps.

In *Being Christian* Rowan Williams has much that is valuable to say about prayer: we should habitually settle and anchor ourselves to be open to self-scrutiny, to be reconciled with others and at peace with them, and to act justly and not be governed by selfish anxiety. In another but similar treatment, prayer is a way of being present in the appointed 'hour' and appropriate season, away from merely chronological time, and deadlines, where time continuously runs out.[11] The authors see prayer as standing outside, tuned to the Creator Spirit, and open to the overtones of praise. Their understanding of appropriate season translates Jesus' 'sufficient unto the day'. They appeal to Rilke's 'angelic' visitations as in his *Book of Hours*, where the poet sees these as alarming because through contemplation they render the world as really present. It is true these authors also speak of God's 'plan' but this refers to no more than fulfilment of the person's 'proper end', something maybe related to what Gerard Manley Hopkins in his sonnet to Henry Purcell calls 'forgèd feature'.[12] It is Hopkins' *'haeccitas'* or 'this-ness' of people as well as the created order.

There is also prayer understood as recollection or bringing carefully to mind. The Christian priest or minister is constantly made aware of needs within and without the active worshipping body, and he or she gathers these up, often by naming those in need in devotional acts of public and private recollection. These acts constitute and promote a community of shared concern that can be realised in active charity. Prayerful recollection is the public and private expression of the concern that each feels for all as 'members one of another'. This is where faithfulness requires a constant recourse to doubt about what is taken for granted. Faith requires doubt in order to locate and expose the rock under the shifting sands. But what might that bedrock be?

We have to return to the governing dichotomy of ruin and restoration and therefore to the governing dichotomy of good and evil. There is a contemporary

---

11   David Steindal-Rast and Sharon Lebell, *Music of Silence: A Sacred Journey through the Hours of the Day*, Berkeley, CA: Seastone, 1998.

12   Gerard Manley Hopkins, 'Henry Purcell', in *The Poems of Gerard Manley Hopkins* (4th edn), ed. W.H. Gardner and N.H. MacKenzie, London: Oxford University Press, 1967, p. 80.

reluctance to talk of good and evil stemming from the ambiguities that inform all our actions and from a chronic fear of appearing to endorse a judgemental attitude based on superior righteousness. Ironically, this chronic fear of superior righteousness is a secular version of Christianity but if we then go on to reject the difference between good and evil and dispense with the very idea of judgement we are lost in a relativistic moral chaos. We have no standpoint. Moreover, we delude ourselves in supposing we can abrogate judgement when in practice we are passionately judgemental. The contemporary world appears to embrace relativism and moral laissez-faire when it is in practice judgemental and condemnatory. Judgement is the foundation of any pursuit of the good whatever the pervasive ambiguities. Abandon it and the only criterion remaining is the all too malleable notion of social utility and that can and does justify evil-doing. Responsibility requires judgements of good and evil and the naming of evil. Eliot wrote in *The Rock* (1934):

> There shall always be the Church and the World
> And the Heart of Man
> Shivering and fluttering between them, choosing and chosen,
> Valiant, ignoble, dark and full of light
> Swinging between Hell Gate and Heaven Gate.
> And the Gates of Hell shall not prevail.
> Darkness now, then
>   Light.[13]

This difference and this confrontation defines the contours of any world claiming to be moral and it is central to Christianity.

Christianity proclaims the possibility of moral change and speaks of 'the renewing of your mind'. To be renewed is to see things from a more comprehensive perspective than narrow self interest. We are born with self-interested instincts whereas to be born again in Christian terms enables us to find ourselves in a more generous understanding of fulfilment. We lose ourselves to find ourselves, as the Gospel expresses it.

But against this vision of restoration stands the ever-present possibility of ruin. We can lose our moral compass to the point where we cannot see what we are doing or where we are going. We are not in our 'right mind'. The divine image in us is not renewed but effaced. Here lies the possibility of a radical evil that eats

---

[13]   T.S. Eliot, from *The Rock* (staged in collaboration with E. Martin Browne and the Reverend R. Webb-Odell), London: Faber & Faber, 1934.

up the self to the point where we fall into an abyss of emptiness where nothing can come of nothing and we diminish by degrees into the hell of non-being. We are to 'take heed unless we fall'. This can come about through a disorder of desire which displaces treasure by idolatry. The New Testament turns on the contrast between the pursuit of our true treasure in heaven and our decline into idolatry. The German language nicely encapsulates the different between 'Schatz', or treasure, and 'ergötzen', or false idolisation, treating as God what is not God. On this the New Testament texts are emphatic to the point of extreme hyperbole. We are to 'seek first the kingdom of God' from which all other goods may flow. It 'profits us nothing to gain the whole world' and lose our soul.

The temptation to idolatry can be traced in all the different spheres of tension generated by Christianity's acute angle of transcendence: the economic, the political, the sexual and the aesthetic. Here I briefly select the aesthetic, especially music as the art I understand best, because as an idol it can eclipse the Christian pursuit of mutual dependence and as a treasure it can illustrate its highest potentialities.[14] Indeed as a treasure it can model the mutual dependence at the heart of the Trinity. It can also model the incarnation, understood as particular embodiment of flesh and blood, here and now. The potential of the aesthetic for exploitation is obvious. It is a branch of witchcraft and false enchantment that turns men into beasts. But there is also a rejection of the idolatrous pursuit of beauty that generates its own aesthetic, for example in Cistercian architecture, and there is a potential for mutual self-giving that models both the incarnation and the Trinity. The very idea of a musical performance depends on watchfulness and attention based on long habituation and dedication. In its realisation it

---

[14]   The difference between the sharp angle of transcendence in Christianity and in Islam comes out in the context of the absolute prohibition of the creation of images of God and of their use in devotion. An incarnational religion is much less likely to give rise to an absolute prohibition of images than a religion of vertical transcendence, although image-making is a marginal element that has developed in some Islamic contexts, for example in Persia, and iconoclasm is a movement that has surfaced in Christianity from time to time, both in the Eastern Church and in the Calvinist Reformation. The degree to which iconoclasm is embraced in Islam can lead to a major confrontation such as we observe at the moment between the secular western concept of the absolute sacredness of art and its artefacts and an Islamist warfare against all kinds of image-making and associated architectural structures that have attracted, or still attract, what is defined as a blasphemous devotion detracting from the absolute transcendence of Allah. A recent television programme on the so-called Islamic State made by the cultural commentator Dan Cruikshank illustrated all too clearly the total incomprehension on the part of a western aesthete towards what a spokesman for radical Islam, Anjem Choudary, had to say about the utter irrelevance of the western concept of art (*Civilisation under Attack*, a documentary film written and presented by Dan Cruikshank, BBC Four, 30 June 2015).

embodies a mutual self-giving of the highest order where each attends with care to the other. It is as near to the mutuality of communion as conveyed in St John's account in chapter 17 of the love shared between the Father and the Son and all who are 'in Christ' as it is possible to imagine. What is true of musical performance can also be true of all kinds of performance art, dance, theatre, pageants and festivals, and most obviously in architecture and in liturgy.[15]

Here we need to turn to the vision of restoration in the Gospels as it expresses and manifests the tension between 'the kingdom' and 'the world'. There is, first of all, the proclamation of 'First Things' already canvassed: the priority of the kingdom over all the limited 'goods' of human life. The Christian angle of transcendence places a question mark against all the spheres of human attachment to the extent that they become exclusive goals and satisfactions. They are not intrinsically other than genuine 'goods', for example devotion to the family, or ordinary material comfort, or aesthetic fulfilment. The governing images of the kingdom and its imperatives are precisely not images of disembodied spiritual atoms but images of fecundity, abundance, mutual care, service and unimpaired communication. These images and imperatives stand in vivid contrast to the pursuit of a single-minded satisfaction of self-centred desire. Those who seek to 'save their lives' will lose the satisfactions they crave while those who 'lose their lives' will discover where 'true joys are to be found'. This paradox is paralleled by the complementary paradox found in the second collect 'for peace' in the service of Morning Prayer. It is that the disciplines of service lead to the achievement of 'perfect freedom'. The paradox is even more striking in the Medieval Latin original 'whom to serve is to reign' – *cui servire regnare est*. These paradoxes may appear to be no more than standard moral truths, mere mottoes, because they have been written into our culture, but they are extraordinarily hard to live by and illustrate the extent to which Christianity runs 'against the grain of the world'. That accounts for the pervasive contrast in the Gospels between narrow and difficult paths that lead to 'abundant life' and wide highroads that lead to destruction.

---

[15] David Martin, 'A Relational Ontology Viewed in Sociological Perspective', in John Polkinghorne (ed.) *The Trinity and an Entangled World: Relationality in Physical Science and Theology*, Grand Rapids, MI and Cambridge: Eerdmans, 2010, pp. 168–83. The fundamental argument of this present book is prefigured in this contribution. In the pages cited I work out the co-determination required by performing 'in concert' and the combination of commonality and difference as providing an analogy of the Trinity. I also discuss the relation between the automatic responses engendered by prolonged practice and the possibility of interpretative freedom, so that discipline and freedom co-inhere.

There is in all this precisely the pursuit of perfection following the command to 'be perfect' with a righteousness that exceeds the moral ostentation of the Pharisees, that historically generates the distinction between the attainments of the average, decent Christian and the saintliness of the pursuit of holiness. Holiness can be pursued in enclaves that seek to enact the imperatives of the kingdom in disciplines of the common life and to create model communities and spiritual families of fathers and brothers, mothers and sisters, from (say) Augustine's fraught experiments in communal living and communities in the Eastern Church consisting as much of 'freeloaders' as virtuosi of asceticism, to the covenant community of the Plymouth Plantation in 1620.[16] However, it is here in the pursuit of the highest ideals that we have to remember the ravages of evil and potentials for corruption. Communities pursuing the perfect are subject to ruin and corruption, in common with all human institutions, and do not provide a viable blueprint for whole societies. It is true that, from time to time, great bishops, law givers and kings have tried to envisage the practices proper to a Christian polity, but the profounder truth is that any attempt to set up the kingdom of God on earth would rapidly and easily degenerate into acts of eschatological violence. In one sense God's kingdom may be an everlasting kingdom 'without end' but its presence lies in wait, a latent pressure glimpsed through image and metaphor. This is another way of saying that Christianity is *not* a political religion whatever its profound political implications. The peace of God is realised only intermittently and symbolically, otherwise there would be no churches or temples or dedicated and delimited sacred spaces or sacramental colonies of heaven like Baptism and the Eucharist, because the light that is now refracted and 'submarine' would be fully present as it is in the concluding chapters of the book of Revelation.

This is not to say that Christians may not seek, in company with others of goodwill, means to negotiate and even reconcile alternative visions and different interests through, say, democratic structures. This enterprise could be seen as deriving from the Wisdom tradition rather than the New Testament which enjoins the spirit of reconciliation without sketching procedural models. Neither the Gospels nor the Epistles are manuals for building Jerusalem.

We now have to set out the imperatives of the kingdom and its governing metaphors and images. I am not expounding the structure of the Gospels, such as the initial proclamation of the kingdom, the various epiphanies of Christ,

---

[16]   Conrad Leyser, *Authority and Asceticism from Augustine to Gregory the Great*, Oxford: Oxford University Press, 2000; for the relaxed ethos of some communities in the Eastern Church see the Epilogue of Brown, *Body and Society*.

the peaceable confrontation of 'kingdom' and 'world' in the Sermon on the Mount, or the transition that begins with the Transfiguration and leads to final confrontation of 'kingdom' and 'world' in the Passion. An account of a repertoire of themes linked by a symbolic logic can begin almost anywhere. The Gospel is not any kind of system to be contorted on a rack of reason but a series of searching probes. We are dealing in pictograms not rationally constructed diagrams and we understand these pictograms through poetic Imagination. Nevertheless, penitence comes very early in the Gospels and it comes first in my thematic repertoire.

Penitence is bound in with judgement and forgiveness. Here we have to remember that consistency requires us to judge others by criteria that we also apply to ourselves: 'Judge not that you be not judged.' As both Testaments make clear we cannot simultaneously pass judgement and insert a clause excepting ourselves. By condemning and passing judgement we inevitably place ourselves under the same condemnation and judgement. The moment we review our past actions and recognise that we could and should have done otherwise we repent and place ourselves in need of forgiveness. This is a moment when we stand back and acknowledge our 'misery' in the original sense of someone in need of mercy and asking for it. To say 'I regret nothing' is to adopt an insouciance outside any imaginable moral universe and to deny human responsibility in principle. It is mere bravado.

Repentance is to recognise that we have let ourselves become enmeshed, mired and trapped by the evil empire of disordered desire. This recognition is the first step to receiving forgiveness. Without judgement and recognition, forgiveness cannot begin its work of acceptance and reconciliation. That is where Truth and Reconciliation commissions have to begin at the political level and the same is true at the personal level. In Christian terms repentance and truthfulness make possible absolution, cleansing and reconciliation. We are washed clean and we are 'covered' by grace abounding, but we also have to face the breakages of faith and trust in which we have been implicated. Mutuality is part of reconciliation: 'forgive us our trespasses as we forgive them that trespass against us'. Moreover, we forgive as much for our own sake as for the sake of the other because to the extent that we harbour thoughts of vengeance we diminish ourselves. This emerged very clearly in the trial in 2015 of 'the bookkeeper of Auschwitz' for complicity in the murder of over a quarter of a million people. There is, first of all, the problem of the insidious slipway that leads by half-noticed steps to entanglement as a minor aide in a wider system of radical evil and of finding a commensurate sentence for a very old man. But beyond that, one of the witnesses for the prosecution offered him forgiveness because for her to contemplate vengeance was to inflict moral damage on herself.

Cleansing after repentance is accomplished in baptism by a passage through water but it is also accomplished in the annual sacrament in Holy Week when Jesus takes a towel to wash the feet of the disciples. This he does to show that the master of all is the humble servant of all and as an act of cleansing. Peter protests that he needs to be washed thoroughly all over, whereas Jesus says that the act of washing feet only acts as a comprehensive act that removes the stains of sin from the whole body.

Here Jesus reverses the order of 'the world' in an act that models the action of God in entering the world as a humble servant rather than as a king seeking to lord it over others in the manner of the Gentiles. If he is also a king he manifests himself as a servant king: the servant of the servants of God. This reversal is at the heart of the Gospel proclamation. Christ turns 'the world' upside down just as his disciples in the Book of the Acts were said to turn the world upside down. The healing miracles make manifest a reversal that includes the disabled: the lame walk and the blind receive their sight, and healing is at the same time a release from spiritual disablement. Christ declares that the first shall be last and the last first and that a 'little child shall lead them'. The stories in the Gospels, whether or not they are strictly parables, constantly reverse the hierarchies of wealth, power and status, so that in the story of the rich man who dines sumptuously and Lazarus the beggar at his door, covered with sores, after death their roles in 'the world' are reversed. Unless one believes that the story depicts the topography of hell, the clear implication is that the chasm separating them in the world is quite otherwise in the sight of God. The story of those who excused themselves from attendance at the great banquet also reverses the 'natural order' because people are brought in off the street to enjoy what the original invitees were ready to pass up.

A related theme concerns the primary pursuit of the lost. The mission of 'the Son of Man' is to seek and to save the lost, the sick and those wounded and 'fallen by the wayside', as in the parable of the Good Samaritan. Apart from illustrating what is required by the second great commandment enjoining love of neighbour, the parable of the Good Samaritan underlines the fund of good will and virtue found among those denigrated as outside the fold of the chosen. The various stories of the Good Shepherd show him as the one who lays down his life for the sheep and who is untiring in the search for those who have in one way or another gone astray. The parable of the Prodigal Son sums up Gospel teaching as much as does the parable of the Good Samaritan. The Prodigal Son has been lost far from home but the moment he seeks pardon and forgiveness he is welcomed with open arms by his father, whose overwhelming joy at his return leads him to 'kill the fatted calf'. This recovery of sonship is a central theme of the Gospel. Those who hear the voice of the Son are given power to enjoy the fellowship with the Father. Out of tiny nuclei in the Gospels can come complete theologies of incorporation in the divine love.

The stories and parables not only reverse the natural order, so that the most unlikely people go first into the kingdom, but they emphasise the need to be ready. At one point Christ says that he has 'piped' but finds his hearers not ready to dance. People are depicted as too sleepy and unprepared to recognise that the moment of decision is upon them and the kingdom of heaven 'at hand'. We easily assume that there is time to consider what really matters when in fact we urgently need to respond here and now. Time is constantly fast-forwarded in the Gospels to dramatise the serious choices which confront us. Infinite postponement and prevarication can lead to spiritual death. The marriage couple are ready for the bridal feast and we need to be ready with our lamps prepared to join them. One of the governing images of the kingdom is the banquet spread for anyone whatever to participate.

If we simply take this governing metaphor of the banquet, especially the marriage banquet, by way of an example, it unlocks the meaning of many of the miracle stories. John's Gospel begins with a miracle of unexpected abundance in the course of a wedding feast. The old wine has run out but the presence of Christ releases the new and overflowing wine of the kingdom. John's Gospel also shares with all the other Gospels the miracle of the feeding of the five thousand. This miracle has been subject to rationalisations about people being stimulated to share provisions they had already brought with them. But if we think of the five thousand as a vast panorama of human need, and then think of the boy as making a tiny offering of his personal possession of loaves and fishes which cannot possibly meet that need except in the hands of the Saviour, then the story is replete with meaning. Christ for his part is empty handed but the offering made by the child shows how much can be multiplied from very little. Again and again in the Gospels what is tiny and insignificant can be infinitely multiplied to feed the world. Christ Himself is the bread of abundant life freely given. If we hoard what we have been given, whether little or much, it will die of inanition. If we haggle and bargain over it we are locked in a limited exchange when we could enjoy the possibility of grace pressed down and running over. Those who enter into the joy of the kingdom are those who recognise the hidden presence of God in any of the needy, despised and rejected. Those who arrive last in the vineyard receive as much as those who have toiled form the beginning.

From the viewpoint of 'the world' everyone is disposable but in the perspective of the Gospel everyone is of infinite worth, so that even the hairs on their heads are numbered. From the viewpoint of 'the world' one may have stored up goods for many years but in the perspective of the Gospel these may vanish in the twinkling of an eye. The vast edifice of the Temple looks so solid and lasting but its time is fast running out. What remains as a rock that cannot be overwhelmed is the saving Word and the loving community of faith, hope and love. Christ is present wherever the agapeic community meets 'in his name'. In the breaking of bread they perpetually renew his presence with them 'to the ending of the age'. That community is brought together for the sharing of gifts: the gifts of the members of his body and the gift of his body for their redemption.

The Christian Eucharist begins with the admission of ruin and the search for grace. It proceeds with penitence and forgiveness and the sharing of gifts in a restored table fellowship and in mutual recognition. The mutuality and the sharing of gifts vertically and horizontally might be illustrated by Francis Quarles in his poem 'My Beloved is Mine and I am His':[17]

> He is my altar, I his holy place,
> I am his guest and he my living food.
> I'm his by penitence, he mine by grace,
> I'm his by purchase, he is mine by blood.
> He's my supporting elm and I his vine:
>> Thus I my best beloved's am,
>> Thus he is mine.

The achievement of recognition might be illustrated by the account of Mary Magdalene at Christ's tomb in a sermon preached by Lancelot Andrewes in 1620 on Easter Day:[18]

> Now *magnes amoris amor* 'nothing so allures, so draws love to it, as doth love itself'. In Christ specially, and in such in whom the same mind is. For when her Lord saw there was no taking away His taking away from her, all was in vain,

---

[17]   Francis Quarles, 'My Beloved is Mine and I am His: He Feedeth among the Lilies', in D.H S. Nicholson and A H E. Lee (eds) *The Oxford Book of English Mystical Verse*, Oxford: Clarendon Press, 1917, p. 21. The poem, based by Quarles on the Song of Songs, was set to music by Benjamin Britten as his Canticle 1 for high voice and piano in 1947.

[18]   Lancelot Andrewes, from 'A Sermon Preached before the King's Majesty at Whitehall on the Sixteenth of April A.D. MDCXX. Being Easter Day', in *Lancelot Andrews: Selected Writings*, ed. P.E. Hewison, Manchester: Carcanet, 1995, pp. 106–7.

neither men, nor Angels, nor Himself, so long as he kept Himself gardener, could get anything out of her but her Lord was gone, He was taken away, and that for the want of Jesus nothing but Jesus could yield her any comfort, He is no longer able to contain but even discloses Himself, and discloses Himself by His voice ...

And now, lo Christ is found; found alive, That was sought dead. A cloud may be so thick we may not see the sun through it. The sun must scatter that cloud, and then we may. Here is an example of it. It is strange a thick cloud of heaviness had so covered her, as see Him she could not through it; this one word, these two syllables, Mary, from His mouth scatters it all. No sooner had His voice sounded in her ears but it drives away all the mist, dries up her tears, lightens her eyes, that she knew Him straight, and answers Him with her wonted salutation, 'Rabboni'. If it had lain in her powers to have raised Him from the dead, she would not have failed but done it, I dare say. Now it is done to her hands.

All with this is turned out and in; a new world now.

Index

repentance: cleansing 120; understanding
119–20
Requiem (Brahms) 86
Requiem Canticles (Stravinsky) 91
reserve, manifestation (Weber) 58
restoration: ruin, dichotomy 114–15;
vision 115–16; impact 117
restored unity, desire 39
Resurrection, story 63
revolutionary activism 77
right mind, absence 115–16
Rilke, Rainer Maria 38, 90–1, 114
Rimsky-Korsakov, Nikolai 90
risk, power (aversion) 28
ritual rectitude, defence 109
Rock, The (Eliot) 51, 115
Romantic style, usage 90
Romanticism: feeling 85–6; individuals,
depredations 93
Rousseau, Jean-Jacques 22–3
ruin: admission 122; restoration,
dichotomy 114–15
Ruskin, John 12
Russia: anti-religious political ideology/
musical power 90; nationalism,
utopian political ideology (union)
93–4
Rutter, John 91

Sachs, Jonathan 107
Sacks, Jonathan 111
sacrifice, commemoration 97
Salt, Titus (vision) 101
Salter, Alfred 101
salvation: history (absence), sin (impact)
36–7; law/grace, cognates 50
Sampson, Carolyn 92
Sapientia (Wisdom) 100
Satan, enemy identification 75
Saul (Browning) 47
scarcity 37–8
Schatz, ergötzen (contrast) 116
Scheherazade (Rimsky-Korsakov) 90
Schnittke, Alfred 91–2

Schönberg, Arnold 91
Schubert, Franz 84, 85
Schubert's Winter Journey (Bostridge) 84
Schumann, Robert 86
Schütz, Alfred 9
Schweitzer, Albert 3
Seasons, The (Thomson) 84
sect/church, tension (history) 74–80
secular pacific sentiment, ethical stance
108
secularisation 18
Seligman, Adam 109–10
Sermon on the Mount 28, 79, 107
servant king, proclamation 19
settled order 27
sex 57; activity, dubiousness 64; bodily
distractions 62; embedding 60;
gender, cultural analogue 57;
power, religion (reflection) 60
sexuality: changes 65; expression, control
65; innocence, stories 59; issues
65–9; weapon, usage 66
Shakespeare, William 51, 84
Shaw, Bernard 106–7
Shostakovich, Dmitri 90
Sibelius, Jean 89
sin 27; consequence 29; disharmony,
comparison 39; forgiveness 31–2;
impact 36–7; law/grace, cognates
50; law, overcoming 53; natural
sufferings/death 35–6; translation (inappropriate abuse) 50
sincerity, critique 109
Sinfonia da Requiem (Britten) 91
social nature: with the grain 57; reserve,
growth 58
social order, representation (modes) 97
social world, conflict (basis) 22
sociology 5; meaning 12; paradox 15–16;
psycho-pathology, relation-
ship 16; reference 8; theology,
similarity 9–10, 17
socio-theology 3–4
soldiers: body language 96; motives 95–6